ALWAYS REMEMBER THIS MOMENT

A True Story About Life, Love and Miracles.

Lots and Lots of Miracles.

Charles Gardner

© 2019 By Charles Gardner
Published by jamisonk.com

For Bob and Tom ~
I'll see you again soon, my friends.

October 2019 - 2nd Printing

"I wanted to thank you for your support and sharing all of the more-than-amazing stories about your own lives, revelations and successes. The second printing of this memoir is to let you know that I have heard you and I will not forget how much of a community this really is. My sobriety continues to be a work in progress; the sepsis I endured in this story has come back to haunt me and caused quite a stir during my travels to Greece. The more I learn the more I have to share!

The kids have graduated school and are finding their own way, and I have semi-retired and moved back to Tennessee to be near to those I love most - my family. " ∎

FOREWORD

There are thousands of stories of people making changes and improving their lives. Each one of those stories is a tribute to what can happen when someone decides to do what is needed to live a better life. This is not one of those stories. This story is about a man who was sick and tired and caught up in every kind of temptation he was brought up to avoid. Life for Charlie not only reached an extreme level of desperation, Charlie was hanging onto that life by a very thin strand of faith and hope and a very powerful God who had plans for Charlie far beyond an early death. He came close, and not just once, but he lived to tell about it and the transformation described in this book.

I met Charlie several years ago when he became part of the NewLife family and I have enjoyed getting to know him better with every encounter. This man who was full of despair and hopelessness is one of the few people I know that puts a huge grin on my face every time I see him walking toward me. He has always filled me up with his stories from his adventure-filled life. If there was ever anyone who needed to write a book, it was Charlie and now he has done it. Now he can share with thousands the great stories of hope and transformation all of us who know and love him have been fortunate to hear.

Charlie's incredible story of transformation is far from a tale of positive thinking and personal empowerment. It is instead just the opposite. This is a story of surrender and coming to accept powerlessness rather than trying harder and tapping into inner resources. And the result is nothing short of miraculous. It is miraculous because a man who had so much, soared so high, and hit bottom so hard, does what truly transformed people does. He gives back. He helps others find the path and process he found. And you can find it too.

No matter what you are going through or what you are experiencing; desperation, hopelessness, confusion, or just in need of a little inspiration to take the next step or the courage to do the next right thing, you will find what you need and more in this remarkable book about a remarkable man. Charlie and his story is a profound example of the message of this book; wherever you are whatever you are going through—always remember this moment! ∎

——— Stephen Arterburn
Author and Host of NewLife "Live"

TABLE OF CONTENTS

CONTENTS

ALWAYS REMEMBER THIS MOMENT

A True Story About Life, Love and Miracles.
Lots and Lots of Miracles.

INTRODUCTION

EARTHQUAKES AND MIRACLES

Where I live, in California, there are earthquakes every day. Today alone (July 1, 2017), there were 18 earthquakes recorded. Most often, they are the sort that are so low in magnitude on the Richter scale that you don't even feel them. But every now and then, there are the ones that make you feel a little dizzy, the lampshade swings a little bit, and you know something is happening. And then, every so often, WHAM! One happens that really gets your attention, and things happen really big. In Southern California, the geology is founded more on sandy material, so the quake comes in a rhythm more like a bowl of Jell-O being shaken. But in Northern California, where the geology is based more on hard stone and granite, these quakes come in the form more like being hit by a train run off its tracks.

Miracles are a lot like earthquakes. They happen every day. Quite often they are happening all around us and go unnoticed. They are so subtle, so much like all else happening in the world, we don't see them. Then there are those that make us pause. "Did that red light that lasted longer than usual keep me out of that accident that just happened ahead?" The opposite happened to me when I decided to pause when I had an opening in traffic, only to end up in my first near death encounter moments later in a head on collision on Devil's Slide near Half Moon Bay.

This is a book of miracles. Some are so subtle you make not see them the first time through. It's also a book about Love. Love of family, friends, and relationships that gave me the will and resilience to live. Often, when I've been absolutely convinced that I am doing what my creator had in mind for me to do, the exact opposite has been true. But I can say that every single time, things have been in play behind the scenes that have unfolded as more of a Divine plan than I could have imagined.

Medically, statistically, I was not supposed to survive. Yet I did. The events leading up to, and what has happened afterwards are chock full of the lessons and miracles that happen to all of us. If there is anything I learned from the experience, is that there is a place where we go after we die, and it is a good place. But it is important that we enjoy the blessing of life that we have been given here on Earth. That we see the miracles that are happening all around us every day.

When pneumonia turns into a blood poisoning called sepsis, the body naturally tries to fight sepsis by shutting off all non-essential organs. In my advanced case, though, everything was shut down. They told me I had 13 strokes as my blood pressures soared off the charts. By some miracle of connections, family members were found and summoned urgently. Considering my condition and the fact I had left a Do Not Resuscitate document, the choices were limited. When the doctors effectively lost all detection of brain activity, the working part of my lungs was less than the size of a finger. On July 25, 2011, they pulled the plug. What happened next is why I wrote this book. ∎

—Charles Gardner, July 1, 2017

1. IT HAPPENED (JULY 2011)

"Life is pleasant. Death is peaceful.
It's the transition that's troublesome" —Isaac Asimov

The piercing wail and flashing red lights served as a rude announcement of the ambulance's arrival. A man in a business suit stood there waving anxiously in the San Francisco Airport parking garage as the paramedics arrived. The person next to him was in obvious distress. The ambulance driver jumped out and surveyed the scene in seconds.

The victim appeared disheveled, apparently ill as he sat on the concrete and propped his back against a tall trash can for support.

"Hey, sir. Are you the one who called for the ambulance?" the driver asked the businessman.

"Yes, I am. I was just going to my car when I saw this man. He seemed ill and incoherent. I called for an ambulance and waited here with him."

"Do you know this man, or did you maybe get his name?"

"No, we couldn't have much of a conversation except that he was looking for his car. Obviously, he didn't get too far." He looked down at his watch. "You got it from here?"

"Yeah. We've got it. Thanks."

The second paramedic brought the power-stretcher around and together the colleagues gently guided the sick man into laying down on the stretcher. After uploading him into the ambulance, the driver turned the siren on and sped off with beds and drips rattling to the Mills-Peninsula Hospital. Every bump the ambulance hit shook the sick man, who incoherently moaned.

The ambulance arrived at the hospital, and the paramedics immediately offloaded their charge to a bed in the Intensive Care Unit. Blood work analysis and x-rays revealed life-threatening conditions.

"Sir, can you tell me your name?" a nurse asked.

"Ch-" was all he could muster.

"Ch..?" the nurse asked. She paused before stating, "Charlie? Is your name Charlie?"

Charlie nodded a weak affirmative and attempted a smile.

"Okay, Charlie, you just hang in there. We're running some tests on you to see what's going on."

Charlie closed his eyes.

The immediate diagnosis was not only the Pneumococcal disease, but also Sepsis. Streptococcus pneumonia bacterium invaded Charlie's lungs, and doctors put in a breathing tube to keep him alive. Sepsis, a blood infection, shocked his organs, and the odds were that it would be terminal.

The attending physician exclaimed, "We have no way of knowing how long this man has been in septic shock. Four hours or fourteen hours? Had we caught it early, he might have had a slight chance at survival. Now, I am not so sure that he will."

The physicians couldn't know that Charlie had been

wandering aimlessly for over twenty hours in that parking garage at San Francisco airport before the businessman found him and called 911.

The doctor induced a coma to keep Charlie alive and out of pain. He was put on a dialysis machine to keep his kidneys active, and a feeding tube was inserted, in addition to an oxygen line.

Charlie's prognosis was very poor. The ICU doctor shook his head left and right during conversations about Charlie, and it was clear that he did not expect his patient to pull through. Charlie was pumped full of morphine while the staff awaited for the inevitable to happen. ■

2. NOT JUST A HEAD COLD

A week prior, Charlie's head cold had turned into a full-blown case of the flu. Although he considered being sick a minor irritation, not feeling well bothered him. However, he wasn't going to let obstacles prevent him from attending his family reunion in Tennessee. It was all planned out, and he had been on board from the get-go. His niece, Becky, would be playing the lead role of the heroine Belle in Beauty and the Beast at their hometown summer theater. The play, and hence the reunion, took place in July, a time of year when Tennessee humidity usually drips off a person. They say you have to take a shower to get new sweat! Already being sick, it wasn't something Charlie looked forward to, but it was family, so he was going to go at all costs.

Becky Gardner as "Belle" in *Beauty and the Beast* ∎

The phone rang, and when Charlie answered it, his brother Ellis cut to the chase.

"Hey, you're still planning to come back for the play and the reunion, right?"

"Yeah, definitely. I've got a bit of the flu, but I'm planning on making it anyway."

"Good, because I wanted to ask you something. Since mom passed away, and you made me executor of your estate, why not bring a written list of all your accounts and passcodes so that I can access them, if I need to, God forbid. You know, like ten to twenty years from now."

Little did Charlie know that Ellis was going to need those codes the very next week.

Until then, the trip went off fine! The play was flawless, leaving   the look of promise for the aspiring careers of Becky and several other young actors and actresses. The weather behaved and was Chamber-of-Commerce beautiful—sunny and warm but not humid beyond endurance. Charlie even felt well enough to play several rounds of golf at Signal Mountain Golf and Country Club, shooting 95 and 97 each time, which was about average for his typical round. Charlie even commented to his brother Ellis that since the weather was so nice at this time of year he should look into buying a place back on the mountain when he gets closer to retirement, so he can come home and golf at the Signal Mountain Country Club, and go fishing in the many creeks and river of the Tennessee River valley. As they were on the 17th hole, Ellis pointed to a house just beyond the green and said, "Oh yes, that one there is yours; the Smiths have owned that house over 30 years and they will be selling one day, and since I will probably be the listing agent, its yours"

The day Charlie headed home, he hadn't realized that his flu had developed into pneumonia. He was also taking a prescription Hydrocodone for lower back and hip pain from surgery a few years back. When coupled with the flu, the condition would flip into something very serious. Flying on an airplane in his condition was dangerous.

As the plane moved to higher altitudes and the oxygen dropped, his blood thinned and his blood pressure rose. The pneumonia went septic and entered his circulatory system. The effect caused Charlie to fall asleep in-flight and wake up six weeks later in a hospital bed. He vaguely remembered being told to get off the plane and telling the ER nurse his name. ∎

3. Vesper Point (July 1969)

Faith is coming to the edge of the light we have, and having the courage to take one more step.

One of Charlie's childhood activities was attending the church's summer camp. Camp Vesper Point, on Lake Chickamauga, was located outside of Soddy Daisy, Tennessee. On the evening of July 28, 1969, when Charlie was thirteen, all the adolescent campers sat around the campfire singing. Moved by this moment, Charlie had a conversion experience. He made the decision to ask Jesus to become his Lord and Savior. The feeling was profoundly transformative as the Holy Spirit filled him with deep joy. Charlie felt the change, body and soul, and knew something enormous and permanent had just happened. A warm serenity signaled that all would be well from that day forward. He felt at one with his Christian family and knew he had a place in eternity; however, he was too young to know there would be potholes along the way. That God is always testing us.

Charlie woke the next morning, still feeling his spirit alive in his physical body. He felt full of joy as he walked around the camp, observing that the sun seemed brighter than normal and the sky boasted a bluer hue than before. He breathed in the cool mountain air, which invigorated all his senses. Never before had he felt so indescribably happy. The surrounding forest of pines flooded his senses with a distinctive evergreen scent. He felt this was a vision of what God had intended for Man to experience when he first made the Earth, before the fall of Adam. By todays standards it would truly be known as a "Claritin Moment."

Seemingly by coincidence that day, the boys and girls were called to the counselors' cabin. They squeezed into the small room to watch a small, black and white, grainy television screen. On that afternoon on July 29, 1969, Neil Armstrong stepped out of Apollo 11's lunar landing module and stepped onto the moon's surface. All of the campers were glued to the television screen as Armstrong said, "That's one small step for man, one giant leap for mankind."

The words went straight to Charlie's heart.

The young man felt confident that his spiritual experience connected him to the moonwalk. It was his earliest epiphany—an awakened curiosity to explore the relationships between science, nature, and God's Universe. When Charlie was younger, he used to look up at the moon and thought: we will be going there sometime soon, maybe within his lifetime. That summer, Charlie also became acutely aware of his intuition. He could feel when something big was about to happen before it did, and he would share these feelings and events with his friends.

The moonwalk also sparked Charlie's deeper interests because of his remembrance of President John F. Kennedy's inaugural speech, in which the President spoke of sending a man to the moon and bringing him back home to Earth. Since then, Charlie held a picture of that event in his mind. He felt beyond amazement in watching his imagined occurrence become real. He knew that God had planned the experience not only for him but for all humans. The connection between Charlie, God, nature and the moonwalk would be engraved in his heart as a miraculous moment.

Another notable event took place at this spiritual encounter. Since the counselors' cabin was so small, the crowded conditions inspired a cute teenage girl named Susan to sit in his lap. Was it hormones, or a sign of his lifestyle to come, or the crowded conditions? They held hands as they watched the moon walk. His step, like his mood, was buoyed up and measurably lighter the rest of the day.

Signal Mountain

Charlie had been born and raised on Signal Mountain, a small town outside of Chattanooga, Tennessee in the foothills of the Great Smoky Mountains. Three thousand people lived in the local community of his childhood in the late 1950s. If an idyllic youth ever existed, then Charlie lived one there on Signal Mountain. Everybody knew each other and he had an active life with a close-knit group of friends. Charlie and his brothers grew up together as adventurous boys hiking and exploring rocks, waterfalls, and caves that carved out the existence of their youth. Natural beauty surrounded their home in southern Appalachia, and the air was filled with a poignant fragrant mist. The trees' natural transpiration created so much vapor in the air that the area came to be named the Smoky Mountains.

The Cherokee brought their cultural heritage to the geographic area by entering the valley from their caves in Alabama. When they saw Lookout Mountain rising majestically above the Tennessee River, they called the area Rock Rising to Point, or Chattanooga, in the Cherokee language..

Charlie and his friends played baseball, tag, and kickball at the nearby ballfield and from September to June, they walked to and from school each day. The area was prone to several natural features that they frequented. Their favorite was Blue Hole, a remote mountain stream that flowed off the back side of Signal Mountain that created a vivid, natural blue swimming hole where the kids went skinny dipping. The hike down to Blue Hole was about a half mile down the ravine off the nearest road. It took Charlie awhile to understand the real meaning of "Blue Hole." When a kid jumped in, he would practically freeze everything off! The distress for guys mildly amused the girls, but they were all friends and understood the results of swimming in the Blue Hole.

Another natural formation and infamous landmark was The Rock, which was about three miles out the bluff from where Charlie lived. The bluff overlooked the Tennessee River Valley. This was a huge outcropping of rocks, which served as gathering spot for locals where bonfires, booze, and music often went on into the night. It wasn't too far from the Mountain Opry house, which had free pot luck dinners and bluegrass music on Friday nights. The Rock was a stopping off point for more nefarious activities. On many a night, cars would be lined up, bumper to bumper, with a large bonfire burning, and the occasional light-hearted music that carried over the valley.

George Hampton, a friend of Charlie's Mom and whom taught mathematics at the University of Tennessee-Chattanooga, was a quirky kind of absent-minded professor who grew his own pot. One time he talked Charlie's Mom into letting him go to Atlanta with him, and they got into all sorts of mischief! George had inherited several properties, and eventually left the house in which he grew up to live closer to the city. He had asked Charlie to keep an eye on the place, not such a good idea, and it quickly became party central for teenagers looking for a place to escape the watchful eye of their parents. The house was right across the street from the Rock. It was where Charlie learned a lot of life lessons, some not the best of lessons, but he felt cool being a part of the scene.

Early Family Life

Charlie was the second of four sons: he had older brother, Tommy, and two younger brothers, Chris and Ellis. Charlie's mother and father divorced when he was nine, and anxiety around money choked the air in the home from that day on. Mary Leavell Gardner, their mom, was an elegant, classic Southern lady with a strong will and a determination to pull herself up by her bootstraps. She had the strong desire to maintain the standard of living she and the boys had grown accustom to.

One morning over breakfast, when tensions were a bit high, Mary stood in the kitchen with her hands on her hips and said to the boys, "Gosh, you boys drink more in milk than the money we get each month." They had an industrial, restaurant-sized milk dispenser that held two five-gallon containers, which the milkman came by to refill twice a week.

Despite some hard times, Mary dedicated her life to raising her four boys, and no one could say she didn't do a great job. Money was tight at first, so everyone pitched in by selling greeting cards door-to-door. Later, Mary sold World Book Encyclopedias and continued the family heritage of being involved in local education. She ended up doing very well, but she always remained dedicated to raising her four boys. Mary and the boys attended the First Presbyterian Church in Chattanooga. The boys' church experiences were positive, and they learned that God was a loving, forgiving God, unlike what many of Charlie's friends had learned about a vengeful, vindictive "scorekeeper" God. Charlie grew up knowing that no matter what you had done, God was always there for you, and His love was unconditional.

The vibe of First Presbyterian Church was that of a loving people that were friendly. The quality of fellowship was high, and people banded together to help each other.

Their Pastor, Ben Haden, was a loving man of the Bible. He started every sermon by reading from the Bible and then related the content to everyday occurrences. Many people in the congregation found emotional, spiritual, and financial help from the church. The congregation believed in and lived by the principles practiced by the early Christian Church in the first century.

As a child, Charlie would see signs of hypocrisy in some people who were outwardly spiritual every Sunday. The child would say, "We all went home to be human again." Even when he was young, Charlie modeled how to live a godly life, and grew to be a keen observer of those who didn't live up to that ideal. First Presbyterian Church welcomed all people and recognized that the original sin of self-will left people broken. The doctrine taught how God wanted to unite us by the sacrifice of Jesus, who died on the cross and bore the burden of collective sin.

McCallie School

Charlie attended the McCallie School for Boys, where his family had a rich tradition and history. As Charlie reached adolescence, he, like his brothers', turned his interests to worldly things like girls, cigarettes, money, and booze. It was not a good spiral for a fourteen-year-old, and it was only a little better as a sixteen-year-old. An early sign of Charlie's emerging alcoholic behavior began to surface in high school when he was driven to be the best athlete. He earned the roles as quarterback on the football team, the captain of the wrestling team, and became the athlete who set the school's records in pole vaulting; yet, if he couldn't reach his goal in a sport, he would just quit and move on.

Under Charlie's helm, the school went undefeated in its 8th grade football season. Later that year, Charlie broke the previous pole vault record, once which had stood for 15 years. By 9th grade, the coach moved Charlie from quarterback to the linebacker to make room for another quarterback, Bobby Goodrich, who was both Charlie's rival and his good friend. While Charlie could admit that Bobby just might have been a better quarterback than him, his reaction, "Screw it. I'll quit," surprised those around him.

Although Charlie spoke those words in anger, his underlying feeling was disappointment, and feeling disrespected burned deeper in his soul than he cared to admit. He was on a championship track in football, and had been derailed, but he would find a way prove himself. As an adolescent, proving himself looked like being rebellious. ■

4. Who Is Charlie?

**The greatest challenge in life is discovering who you are.
The second greatest challenge is liking what you find.**

The rebellious attitude of his youth would be exactly what Charlie would need when later facing his health crisis. When he entered the hospital, the doctor performed what is commonly known as a "wallet biopsy" and discovered a wallet with a business card and the unknown man's name, Charles Gardner. The hospital staff discovered that Charlie was a project manager for Kiewit Infrastructure West, with the Northern California District office in Fairfield, California. When a nurse attempted to call the Kiewit office, the receptionist, Janet, directed the call to Charlie's immediate supervisor, area manager Dave Hazen. Dave coordinated with Patti Llamas, the Director of the Human Resources Department. They learned that Charlie's listed next of kin was his mother, Mary Leavell Gardner of Signal Mountain, Tennessee.

After dialing Charlie's mom and finding neither an answer nor a way to leave a message, Dave had to find another option. What neither Dave nor Human Resources knew at the time was that Charlie's mom had passed away several years earlier, yet Charlie had never updated the contact information. Concerned about Charlie, the firm's district manager, the area manager, and Charlie's supervisor cloistered in Patti's office.

Charlie's boss was in tears. "I know he's got brothers back in Tennessee, but I have no idea what their names are. How do we find them?"

As if an angel whispered in her ear, Patti said, "I know. Charlie was at the stockholder's dinner this past year with his Russian girlfriend. Why don't we see if we have a guest list from the stockholder's dinner? People registered for that black-tie affair." They examined the list and found Charlie's girlfriend's name, Marina Dorovskikh Cottle.

"That's great. But how do we find her?" asked Charlie's boss.

Patti answered, "Well, let's find her on Facebook. Everyone's on Facebook."

As luck would have it, they found Marina on Facebook, and she had listed her work location, another local hospital. Patti looked up and called Marina at the hospital. Marina was working that day and a message came to her to call Patti at Kiewit.

Marina called, and Patti asked, "Do you know Charlie Gardner?"

"Yes."

"Well, I am Patti at the Kiewit office where Charlie works."

"Has something happened?" Marina asked, immediately concerned.

"Well, yes, Charlie is very sick and is in the hospital on the peninsula."

"Is he in danger?"

"Yes, the situation is life-threatening. We want to notify Charlie's family members, but don't know how to reach them?"

"Wait, first tell me what's wrong with Charlie? Which

hospital is he in?"

"I'm sorry, I wish I knew. The hospital could not tell us his location or condition, only that it is very serious and they need to contact his next of kin right away.

"Ah, okay."

Charlie's girlfriend, Marina, had migrated to the United States from Russia in 2003 and met Charlie on a dating website. By moving to a new country, staying busy with work, and going to college, she was left with little time to get acquainted with new people. Marina decided to try a dating website, and though many different men responded, Charlie stood out to her. He was persuasive when he asked Marina to dinner. Though shy and new to the dating scene, she took a deep breath and said, "Okay!"

For their first date, Charlie chose the Steamers Grill House in Los Gatos. Marina's first impression of her date was of a tall, big guy with a bright smile and friendly eyes. She thought the in-person Charlie was more handsome than the online Charlie. She found him to be gentle in his conversation and pulled no punches during dinner. He told her he was in recovery from alcoholism, a disclosure that startled Marina.

"I grew up in a different society with different traditions about disclosures. Some things you might want to keep secret," she said. "I have not dated anyone in this country because of my time commitments, but I was interested in and confident about you."

She said yes when he asked, "Do you want to meet me a second time?"

For their second date, Charlie cooked a delicious dinner of barbecued ribs. He explained that being born in Tennessee meant he knew how to cook a rack of ribs smothered in homemade barbecue sauce. Over time, Charlie shared more of his personal story: church, his previous marriage, and raising his twin stepchildren, Kian and Kyla. That touched Marina's heart deeply, and their relationship developed into an active friendship, and they became traveling companions.

As a nurse, Marina could contact others and rapidly found out that Charlie was at the Mills-Peninsula Medical Center in Burlingame. When her thirteen-hour shift ended at 7:30 that night, she drove straight to the hospital while still in her scrubs. The summer evening was so splendid that Marina breathed deeply to reduce her anxiety while covering the forty-five miles from Los Gatos. When she entered the hospital, people nodded in greeting, thinking she was one of the employees. She walked into ICU and asked, "Can you explain what's happening with Charlie Gardner?"

She followed the ICU nurse into Charlie's room and panicked when she saw him on the bed with all the tubes in him. She whispered, "Oh my God, what's going on?"

"Somebody saw him leaning deliriously against a trash can in the airport parking garage. He was in the parking garage at San Francisco airport trying to find his car."

"Then what?" Marina asked.

"Whoever found him called 911. The paramedics brought him here because Mills-Peninsula was the closest."

"Oh, my God. This is just crazy." Marina saw her six-foot-two boyfriend of 250 pounds laying pale and frail with tubes everywhere. She whispered, "Come on, Charlie. What are you doing here?"

A female doctor approached and explained: "I'm going to tell you what's going on since you're in the field. I can tell you that he has really bad pneumonia." The x-rays the nurse showed Marina displayed his lungs in a white out, which meant extensive inflammation occurred. The doctor continued, "He's in septic shock. All his organs are in failure, hence all these tubes. We are keeping him alive through dialysis because his kidneys are failing, and of course there's the feeding tube as well as a ventilator for breathing."

Marina sat, holding back tears, with Charlie and watched the slight inhale and exhale of his breath. Every time a nurse came in to provide mouth care or check on Charlie, the nurse spoke to him although they believed him to be entirely unconscious. "Charlie, we're going to clean your mouth." "We're going to turn you over." "I'll give you a bed bath."

Marina liked and appreciated their standard of care.

Next, a doctor entered the room and looked Marina in the eye. "We can't find anyone who knows him. Do you know any of his family members?"

"Well, yes. I know his ex-wife, Kerri, but not where she lives. I will try to track her down tonight."

Marina went home and wasted no time searching on the computer for his brothers' names or Kerri. She found nothing. Next, she searched Facebook and found one of Charlie's three brothers and sent him a message: Can you please call me at this phone number. But he didn't call.

When Marina returned to Charlie's side on the second night after working her shift, the doctor found her and asked, "You know we found his phone, but we cannot unlock it. By chance, do you know the password?"

"No, I don't know it."

"Well, we tried so many times and just failed."

Marina tried to contact a mutual friend who lived in Lake Tahoe, where Charlie had a vacation home. Bill Basset was a longtime friend from Charlie's days in Southern California. Marina called his shop at the Lake, but found Bill was on a surfing trip in Sumatra in French Polynesia. The best she could do was send him an e-mail and hope he would check it.

Then Marina remembered a clue. Every time Charlie and Marina traveled together, they liked to get two-hour massages. Recently, Marina went to the Perfect Day Spa that allocated massages by hours. She remembered the code because she had to enter it to gain access to a health spa they shared.

"Oh, my God. I do remember his code - 6 011."

The jubilant doctor and Marina finally unlocked Charlie's phone and found the numbers for his brothers and his ex-wife, Kerri. First, Marina called Chris Gardner, who in turn called Tommy Gardner, the eldest, then Ellis, the youngest. She called Charlie's best friend Roger Berry, who took the next flight out of Phoenix to the Bay Area.

Marina started coming to the hospital a bit later after work, and she met all of Charlie's brothers as they arrived to be Charlie's side. Each brother arrived individually, and what they saw entering the ICU shocked them. Charlie was still unconscious as he lay in bed attached to machines that provided all the life sustaining services for his brain and body. From that first night, in the Intensive Care Unit, one person or more was with Charlie. There were always visitors in his room, always. The word had spread, "Charlie is dying."

Chris Gardner Rallied the Brothers

When Chris, one of Charlie's younger brothers, received Marina's first call, it was about noon in Colorado, where he was attending a business conference. At first, he wasn't fully aware of how dire the situation was, as Marina told him only that Charlie was in the hospital. Chris assumed that it was not an urgent matter and that doctors would take care of Charlie. But then Marina called a second time only an hour later, saying "Chris, look, I've talked to the doctor, and Charlie will probably not make it. You need to come here." Chris had to hear it that way to get him to act quickly.

In response to Marina's call for action, Chris first informed the eldest brother Tommy, who worked for the Department of Navy in Washington, D.C. Next, he spoke with the youngest brother, Ellis, a realtor who lived in Signal Mountain, Tennessee.

Chris later received a call from the brothers' mutual friend, Roger Berry, who was first to arrive at the hospital, and was told, "Tell your brothers if they want to see Charlie while he is still warm, they need to come now!" Chris left work, went home, booked a flight out of Denver, and arrived in San Francisco several hours later.

Roger Berry had arrived two hours earlier and he picked up Chris at the airport. As they drove back to the hospital, Roger explained what they knew about Charlie's condition at the time: "I understand from the paramedic's report that he was delirious when they picked him up in the parking lot, but he could mumble answers to a few questions. However, he lost consciousness immediately after he was delivered to the hospital. By the time Roger arrived, Charlie was not communicating because he was comatose."

Mostly, the medical staff thought Charlie was dying, and the family members needed to be there. The reports weren't positive in the least: Charlie was in a dire situation. Although he didn't quite seem to be dying yet, Roger and Chris felt they were waiting only for the when, not if.

Charlie Always Said He Was Fine

"When Chris called, I was stunned," Ellis Gardner, the youngest brother, told Marina. He was still adjusting to the sudden reversal of events. Charlie had just visited his family to watch Ellis's daughter star in a leading role in a local play.

"Charlie spent a couple of days around July Fourth in bed at his home in Montara, California," he continued. "Then, he called me later and said that he was coming, that he felt better. He arrived on July seventh. We even played golf that day, visited, and went to the Playhouse production the following night." Ellis sat down in a chair as he continued telling Marina what he remembered about Charlie's trip. "While we were playing golf, Charlie was already sick with the pneumonia, but didn't know it. He did comment that the weather was so nice at this time of year, that he confessed to be 'checking it out' as he was considering buying a house somewhere back on the mountain. We were on the 17th hole and I pointed over to a house by the green and said, "I've been keeping my eye on that house for you, the Smith's have been in there for 30 years and they're going to sell someday. You will love it because it's on the golf course, walking distance to the clubhouse, and it has a swimming pool." He responded, "Let me know when it comes up for sale, and maybe I'll buy it!

"Charlie had a cold before he came. While he was there, he was coughing through the evening, and sucking down cough syrup. But Charlie being up at night is not an unusual thing. Every time I asked him how he was or if he needed anything, he replied with his typical Charlie response, 'No I'm fine. I'm all right.'"

Marina nodded as she listened to Ellis. His eyes teared up as he continued.

"I put Charlie on the airplane on Sunday morning, July eleventh, around nine that morning. He was headed to San Francisco, like they said, with a connection in Atlanta, Georgia. Apparently, he fell asleep waiting for the connection and missed the flight."

Somehow, only to be pieced together later, Charlie made it to San Francisco. "The irony is that Charlie had supervised the construction of the Rental Car facility nearby, and probably felt like he was walking around at the job site." Marina explained. "But, he was deathly ill. Someone found him and called an ambulance, and he ended here."

Ellis nodded at Marina. He had learned about Charlie's illness when he checked his phone upon awakening one morning. Marina had left a message for him at 2 am, after she spoke with Chris earlier that night. Immediately, Ellis called Chris and learned that Charlie was in the hospital and he was not doing well. Chris was headed there as he spoke.

When Chris told his brothers that he was on his way, Ellis trusted the situation would be in good hands. Chris handled stressful situations well, and Ellis respected that. Ellis himself knew that he could complete business and family events around his two teenagers, and he then made it to the hospital one week later. Chris and Roger kept him informed of Charlie's condition.

Roger Berry Investigated

Roger received a phone call from Rena Basset, who had left a message for her husband, Billy Basset, while he was in French Polynesia. Billy did not know what hospital Charlie was in, but the message he received from Marina was that Charlie's situation was dire. Roger had a cousin in the Bay Area, so he called her and received a list of the most likely hospitals near San Francisco. The first one he called was Seton–Daly City, but no one with the name Charlie Gardner was admitted. The next hospital he called was Mills-Peninsula, and when asked who he was, Roger halfway lied and said he was Charlie's brother. That Roger was a brother was true. Charlie, Roger Berry, and Billy Basset were best of friends in their early working years in Dana Point, California. The Gardner clan did unofficially adopt Roger and Billy as "Gardner brothers." In answer to Roger's question about Charlie Gardner being admitted, "Yes, he's here," they said.

Roger asked, "What's wrong?"

"Due to HIPPA policies, we can't disclose that information."

Roger followed up with the question, "Okay, I understand. Just tell me, is it serious enough that I should come tonight?

"Yes," came the reply.

Roger immediately booked a passage to fly into San Jose since it was most convenient and affordable. He then called and alerted Kerri, Charlie's ex-wife, and Chris Gardner. Arriving in San Jose airport with a receipt for his reserved rental car, he was dismayed to find all the rental car companies closed for the night. Walking to the garage, Roger saw an Alamo Rental employee driving out of the garage. He stopped her, and talked her into returning and opening up again to allow him to pick up his car and get to the hospital.

Roger was the first one to arrive in Charlie's room in the ICU. During the first five days, he stayed in the ICU with Charlie and then with Chris when he arrived. Watching a comatose brother hooked up to the machines that operated his body's functions was gruesome. The thought of Charlie dying alone bothered Roger particularly. Every day, along with the doctor, Roger reviewed the lung X-rays and saw how the infection appeared as a white mass. Charlie was on one hundred percent oxygen, and his oxygen saturation was eighty, which is considered very low. His body appeared as if it were going to die right then.

Roger kept in touch with Tommy and Ellis via phone and updated them on the situation, even though Charlie wasn't getting better. Roger explained, "The doctors could take Charlie off the drug Propofol, which kept him in a coma; they did a pain test by shoving a key into the bottom of his foot. There's zero reaction. Nothing!"

When the doctor completed an EEG for brainwaves, and the nurse said to Roger, "There's nothing there. He's done," she shouldn't have said it because it wasn't the official result, but she was kind to do so. Now that Roger knew where the situation was headed, he had to start his new job back in Phoenix, and then he would return to be by Charlie's side. However, Roger wasn't the only one who didn't want Charlie to die alone.

Bill Basset Arrived from Indonesia

Roger updated Bill by phone, "Listen, Charlie's not going to make it. There's nothing you can do. I just felt you needed to know how serious the situation became."

"We've have been friends for a very long time. I am coming anyway."

Roger tried to make it easy for Bill. He knew Bill was

following his dream and was spending his fiftieth birthday by a planned surfing trip to Indonesia, where the best surfing in the world takes place. His vacation destination was the island of Sumatra. He stayed there for a few days and then boarded a ninety-foot vessel with nine other Hawaiian guests. Ten people on the boat were going to live aboard for twelve nights and thirteen days. They went ninety nautical miles off Sumatra to a chain of the best surfing islands in the world.

"There was no cell service," Bill told Roger. "I was completely detached from the outside world for most of this trip, and that was the purpose."

On about the seventh day, Bill and the crew of travelers came to an island where they got gasoline and water in a small village of Indonesians. This was the first time he had been on land in a week. He walked around, stretched, and was ready to surf some more. Then his cell phone rang, but it wasn't Roger. Rather, it was his wife, Rena. She called to update Bill about some repairs on the store, as well as to tell him about Charlie. The news was crushing. Of course, I'm thinking how do I get off this boat? How do I get on a plane? How do I get home?

"I just had to have some level of acceptance about the conditions in which I found myself. I'm with nine other people. They've paid a good price for this adventure," Bill told Rena.

He couldn't jump on a plane. So, he spent the rest of his time surfing and when he got back in Kuala Lumpur, he got another call from Rena at his hotel updating him on Charlie.

Bill didn't get back home to the United States until late in the evening. He crashed and fell into a dreamless sleep but he was awake early the next morning as he wanted to see Charlie. Ellis was at the hospital and he called Bill before he left the house in the morning.

"Billy you really don't need to come today," Ellis said.

"What do you mean?"

"I want you to remember Charlie for who he was."

"Well, I came all the way from Indonesia to see him. I'm coming."

"Really, how do you want to remember Charlie?"

"You know what? I'm coming, regardless. I don't care. I will be there in four hours!"

Bill and Rena drove the 200 miles to Mills-Peninsula Hospital in Burlingame in about two-and a-half hours. Walking into Charlie's hospital room with the tubes and machines was shocking for Bill to see. Because of organ failure, the dialysis couldn't keep up, and Charlie was all swollen up like the Pillsbury Dough Boy, and didn't look like Charlie at all. He moved to Charlie's bedside and started talking to his old friend as though he was sitting there looking back at him and ready to engage in conversation.

"I'm here Charlie. I'm here."

At one point, Charlie's eyes opened a little bit. Bill thought that maybe he followed his movement. Then he doubted himself. Charlie just might wake up. Of course, that didn't happen in all his wishful thinking. The experience of seeing his normally robust friend lying comatose shocked him, yet he felt so strongly that Charlie was there, was awake, and that gave him a little bit of hope.

Afterwards, Bill and Rena had lunch as Ellis filled them in about what they believed happened and how the doctors thought Charlie was dying or dead. The situation was very grim, but, Bill still felt strongly that there was more to the story...so much so...that he was driving to San Francisco at least twice a week, sometimes three times a week, for several weeks to see Charlie. Somehow Bill just intuitively knew his lifelong friend was still there and he was not giving up on him no matter what the "professionals" said.

"If there was any silver lining in this situation," Bill later told Rena as they were out driving one day. "I think it was that Charlie had never been alone. Each of his brothers, as well as Roger, other friends, and I rotated in-and-out on a schedule." Beyond the men in Charlie's life, the women and kids—Marina, , Kerri and the twins, Kyla and Kian—and other long-time friends from his recovery network, his pastor and church friends—they we were all there.

Each one of them unitedly held a vigil for six weeks, as if they could, through their physical presence, will him to return to life. Maybe! Churches and recovery groups across California, Arizona, Texas, and Tennessee, even the Oakland Interfaith Gospel Choir were praying earnestly for God's Will and healing."

Then, the time came for the decision. The doctors wanted to turn off the machines. Bill asked, "What do you mean you're going to turn off the machines?" He couldn't think much of that option.

Returning to the Hospital Scene

Before Chris Gardner left Colorado to fly to Charlie's bedside, he called Kerri and explained Charlie's dire situation. Charlie and Kerri had been to that hospital before, and she was still on the record as being his wife. She learned that after the ambulance delivered Charlie to the hospital, and before he went comatose, a medic asked if he wanted them to call his wife.

His response was no, and then he went into a coma. Kerri likely knew that Charlie was thinking that he was going to be okay—that he didn't want to bother anybody, and that he would cause undo worry for others. Kerri just didn't want Charlie to be alone or to die alone.

Kerri did not know that Marina was at the hospital, and when she called, the ICU nurse answered. Kerri explained who she was and that she wanted to bring the children to see their dad.

"Absolutely not!" The nurse was adamant, noting that under no circumstances would Kerri be able to get anywhere near Charlie.

As it turned out, the medic who had asked the delirious Charlie if he should call his wife, had then written down in bold letters No Wife. Kerri could imagine how the nurse saw the situation: Oh my God, the ex-wife wants to come in here, and we've got his girlfriend sitting here. Boy what a disaster that's going to be!

However, Kerri and the twins could get permission from Charlie's brothers to go into the ICU room and for the twins to see their dad.

Kerri and the Twins

Before Charlie and Kerri first met, they shared the same friends in their small town and ran into each other at meetings and social functions and started to notice each other. Kerri watched him from the sidelines at these gatherings, once getting his attention by commenting that he needed to quit smoking. She watched him through the time when he lost his job and was impressed with how he handled the situation with positivity and cheer, a sign of good character. She noted that Charlie was true to his word, and that people could depend on him. As Kerri learned more about Charlie's resilience and can-do attitude, she liked what she saw.

A year of casual encounters went by before they started dating in 1998. At the time, Kerri had two-year-old twins, Kyla and Kian, from a previous relationship where the father was not present and did not want to be involved. Thus, Kerri was a single parent of twins twenty-four hours a day, seven days a week. Her sole focus, besides work, was her children. She really didn't have time for a relationship and wasn't expecting one, but when it evolved, she was delighted

Tommy Gardner: I Want to See for Myself

Tommy is the first-born of the Gardner brothers. After playing football for the Naval Academy and after a naval career, he became and still is a mechanical/nuclear OGA professional in Washington DC.

When Chris called Tommy and he heard the words "Charlie is in the hospital," he was shocked.

'No, that can't be right. He was just in Tennessee," Tommy replied.

"He came back from Tennessee," Chris explained, "and nobody had heard from him. He had a bad cough, and he'd been playing golf with Ellis. He was taking Tylenol, then Tylenol with codeine. All of that was masking his pneumonia, and he became septic with pneumonia. His condition is pretty serious."

Ellis had put Charlie on a flight back home from Chattanooga. He knew that Charlie missed the layover in Atlanta, but that he boarded the next flight, for which there was a sixty-dollar change fee. Now, Charlie would say, 'Yeah, well I missed my flight. But I met this Saudi Arabian Sheik, and he took me to San Francisco on his private jet.'"

Charlie would swear that happened. His mind told him that happened, but it didn't.

"He got on a Delta flight and made it as far as the San Francisco airport parking garage. His bags came in, and he never picked them up, said Chris.

"Let me check my work schedule, and I'll call you back. I'll be there as soon as I can." Tommy started finalizing his plans.

Ellis Arrived Next

Charlie's youngest brother Ellis arrived at the hospital. Charlie was stable and still in a coma. Ellis held Charlie's durable power of attorney and wanted to be present for Charlie as decisions would need to be made. Luckily, Ellis, as a residential realtor, could work from anywhere. Most of the business was talking with other realtors, dealing with emails, questions, and leads online. Since he had the freedom of movement, he moved his portable office to Mills-Peninsula Hospital.

After losing their mother, and having been the only son local to Signal Mountain, Ellis also held her durable power of attorney. Her health issues incapacitated her for several weeks, and Ellis handled her affairs, which was, he believed, why Charlie asked him to handle his affairs when they played golf the previous week. Now, with Charlie being in a coma, Ellis was in constant communication with Dr. Steyer, the physician in ICU.

Ellis discovered that Mills-Peninsula Hospital was a brand-new facility and had opened just one week before Charlie arrived via ambulance. The state-of-the-art hospital was fully staffed but under-utilized. Family members and friends could go to the intensive care ward and stay by Charlie's side, with some staying overnight. The doctor wasn't in a hurry to move Charlie out of the ICU because he was the only patient. The other nine beds boasted new, clean sheets, but were empty.

Along with Roger and Chris, Ellis learned of the intricacy of Charlie's complications.

"His walking pneumonia is so severe that oxygen levels in his lungs dipped close to zero," Dr. Steyer explained. "Pneumonia filled his lungs with mucus and his body is drowning, so to speak. Charlie's pneumonia turned septic, which caused his lungs to swell. His body and brain shut down with everything else except his heart and lungs. He can't move his arms or legs."

The neurologist continued to explain that when the brain faces this type of massive challenge, it insulates itself and goes into hibernation. In Charlie's case, the massive sepsis infection was in both his blood and his brain. The doctors told Charlie's family that if the sepsis was not diagnosed within the first four hours of onset, there was a one-in-four chance of survival. After four hours, sepsis is nearly always fatal with symptoms of fever, disorientation, and flu-like conditions, just like the ones Charlie was admitted with.

If the doctor's prediction was correct, Charlie's survival chances were slight at best. In fact, when his brothers first saw him, he had been pumped up with morphine to battle the infection while inducing the infamous Michael Jackson drug Propofol to maintain him in a coma." While his brothers hoped for the best, they could only relay to friends that hope for Charlie's recovery was fading.

His family would be faced with the tragic choice. Should they authorize the doctors to pull the plug and end Charlie's life? Continue to pray for a miracle? In any event, they would never forget the daredevil risk-taker who grew into an intelligent, empathetic man with a generous, caring heart. As a child and a teen, Charlie had already faced more than common challenges that shaped his character. He had been through a lot to reach this point where so many embraced and loved him. ■

•   https://www.yahoo.com/gma/sepsis-blood-poisoning-kills-thousands-no-drugs-help-224109669--abc-news-wellness.html

5. Tommy Sets the Stage

"Don't be afraid to give up the good to go for the great"
—John D. Rockefeller

One afternoon while Tommy and Marina sat with Charlie, he told her more about Charlie. "Charlie was a great athlete as a child and as a teen. You should have seen him. Although I was a year and a half older than him, he was a far superior athlete. The coach moved him from the youth league baseball, the minor leagues, up to the major leagues a full year ahead of me. He had excellent eyesight in that he targeted the ball and hit it every time, compared to my constant whiffing because I couldn't see the ball." He smiled at the memory and Marina encouraged him to continue.

"We spent most of our days outside on a ball field because we lived right next door to Norris Field on Signal Mountain. There were always guys outside playing baseball, football, or even basketball. All the local neighbors turned out to watch the games and cheer us on. We played the coal miners' sons, and let me tell you—they were a tough bunch. They lived on one side of Division Street. Our family lived on the opposite side of the street, which ran all the way through town. On our side of the Division Street neighborhood, younger workers lived on the mountain while their parents worked down in Chattanooga Valley. We realized that Division Street had a true division. But, I really didn't comprehend the irony of the name of that street until later. Yet, like kids on a team, all we cared about was whether one could throw, hit, or catch the ball. We didn't care what the family did or where they came from unless they could tackle the kid with the ball! "Charlie quarterbacked for the seventh and eighth-grade teams, and I don't think they ever lost. He was undefeated as the quarterback in eighth grade. He was also an accomplished wrestler. I don't think he lost any sporting events in junior high school. Charlie could have had an athletic scholarship to any university he wanted to attend. Amazingly, it was his three brothers who earned athletic scholarships." Tommy shook his head and looked down at his now nearly grave brother. "Chris went to wrestle at Auburn. Ellis went to play football, wrestling, and track at Georgia Tech. I went into the Navy. Charlie? Well, he went to Arkansas and became the 'Bud Man on Campus' for the Budweiser distributor. It was a dream job for any college boy, and it suited his personality well as a remarkable people person."

Marina looked down at Charlie and wondered how this notorious athlete and man could now be laying hooked up to tubes, bloated and barely alive, maintained by intubation, a feeding tube, and extreme medication.

Dream Home and Uncle Zeke's Car

Tommy liked talking to Marina. She was sweet and listened to every word he spoke. She hadn't come from a family like theirs and the dynamics were intriguing to her.

"Our earliest memories as kids were of living in a house that my father designed when I was seven and Charlie was five," Tommy stated. "The home sat right on a beautiful point of the mountain with a spectacular view of the Tennessee River below. Dad's design of the basement was unique for a home. It was essentially a three bedroom, child's recreation center. There were three rooms, one for each of the first three brothers. There was a restroom with three toilets in a row, and then three shower stalls stood in a row. The feeling of the basement was like an athletic dorm with a giant playroom or recreational area.

"Then, baby brother Ellis was born, and strangely, six-year old Charlie just adopted Ellis. He wanted to make sure he took ownership of this little child, and mother was scared to death that he was going to drop Ellis. Dad was supportive and wanted to encourage that kind of help and nurturing when they brought Ellis home from the hospital. Charlie confidently strolled into the house with Ellis, and just as confidently handed him right back to mother, saying, 'I've done what I was going to do. Here ya go.'

"Since I was the older brother, our Uncle Zeke (real name Ira Ellis Castor Wister Smith III) passed his nineteen sixty-five Ford Fairlane on to me. Uncle Zeke was what the family called a character in the kindest of terms. According to the family story, Zeke had this older sister, and his mother and father owned a fruit plantation out in California. This was during the Caesar Chavez days of political unrest on the plantations. The uprising was from laborers who set fire to the three-story mansion and the plantation. High winds scattered the fire. Zeke's mother and father, who survived by making it out of the house, were sleeping on the first floor. The older sister and baby Zeke were on the third floor. The parents went back inside to look for the children. Dad took Zeke and threw him out of the third-floor window. The firemen, who had just arrived, caught the baby in a blanket. Mom took the older sister and tried to get out of the house. Unfortunately, neither Mom, Dad, nor the sister made it out alive. At the age of one, Zeke was already both an orphan and also a multi-millionaire. Moreover, his legal name was Ira Ellis Castor Wister Smith III, which was conducive for eccentricity.

"From the family's viewpoint, we loved our eccentric uncle, who attended seven different colleges and was clearly a creative soul. Eventually Zeke directed plays in New York City and became very close friends with Beverly Sills, the opera singer. But, we didn't realize until later, Zeke was gay — and homosexuality was never discussed back then. However, our mother fully understood and was very close with Zeke. He was influential in teaching us to dress properly, like tucking in shirts. He was influential in deciding where we had dinner because Zeke specialized in culinary arts.

"So, anyway, Zeke gave me his Ford Fairlane when I turned sixteen, and he bought a new Mercedes. Charlie had to scrape together enough money from a summer job and bought his own fifty-six Chevy, which was a junk car of sorts. One evening, my Ford wouldn't start, and I had a date. Charlie didn't have anything to do, so I told him, 'Hey, Charlie, I need your car. I'm late to pick up my date.'

'No. I might use it.'

'Well I need a car.' Mom was out working, selling World Book encyclopedias door-to-door successfully. She worked fourteen to sixteen hour days just trying to put food on the table.

'No. I need the car.' Charlie insisted.

'You're not using it. I'm taking it.' Well, that set Charlie off. He followed me outside and we got into a fight, the worst and the last we ever had. Charlie was such a superior athlete that he could have beat the devil out of me.

"I wasn't any bigger than he was at sixteen, but I was a little bit faster. I was picked on all the time, and I was fighting all the time, as a kid. Charlie was a good athlete and a great guy, but no one wanted to fight him. But we fought that day to the point Charlie took the tire iron out of his car and it almost turned awful. When mom came home, she made Charlie give me his keys, so I went on my date. We both realized from that point on that we did not like to fight." Tommy looked at Marina, who was looking at Charlie laying in the bed.

Hard Working Mother

"You boys have quite the bond, don't you?" Marina asked.

"Yeah, it grew a lot over the years and through the tough times. Tough times can pull a family apart or strengthen the bond. With us it strengthed," said Tommy. "When we boys were younger, dad was a traveling salesman. One day, he suddenly up and left and didn't leave any money for the family. Mom had to fend for herself, take care of the house, find a job, and raise four boys. She took a job selling World Book Encyclopedias, and she was a top salesperson, as it turned out.

"When she left the house to go to work, Mom left food for us, or she would come home, cook, and go right back out again. I pitched in as much as I could. One year, I made three hundred dollars selling Christmas cards door-to door-between Thanksgiving and Christmas. No neighbor wanted to say no to a smiling seven-year-old. The next year Charlie tried selling and was successful. Well, Mother decided she could sell greeting cards, and still raise the kids, and still make a little money. Then selling greeting cards turned into selling wedding invitations, which had a much better profit margin. Then wedding invitations turned into selling World Book Encyclopedias.

"Mom had such a knack for sales that she went from doing sales to being the district leader, and then she became a regional head. That's when she started making a very good salary. She would knock on a door and talk to somebody for three hours and never mention World Book. She asked questions: How are you doing? How are the kids? How are their grades? Do you like to read with them? She knew people in all ten counties around us, and she went to every door. She had a strategy and a plan. At the end of the two-hour conversation, she would say, 'Oh by the way, I think little Johnny might benefit from having a set of World Books. You know, education's important. If you want to give him a chance to get ahead in life, he needs to read these.'" Tommy laughed. "She really knew how to be genuine, which made her so great at sales."

It's in The Genes

"I think Charlie picked up some of Mom's charisma being around her and from his kinship to her side of the family," Tommy said.

Marina nodded in agreement, "Yeah, he must have. It's what drew me to him in the first place."

"Did you know that his middle name is Moses, and mom was Mary Leavell Moses, so he's associated being closer to a Moses than a Gardner. Our grandfather was Charles Leavell Moses, Jr. and our great-grandfather was Charles Leavell Moses, a Congressman from the state of Georgia. Back then you didn't get elected through ballot voting; the process was simpler. People gathered together around the courthouse and said, 'Hey, Charles, it's your turn to go.' People took turns because nobody wanted to go to Washington, D. C. mostly because you couldn't fly home on weekends. Rather, Charles came home once a year during the Congressional recess. Usually, nobody served more than one term because what Southerner would choose to spend more than two years up in Yankee land, which is what D. C. was called back then. In fact, Charles Leavell served two terms in Congress because no one else wanted to take his place.

"At the turn of the twentieth century were people whose parents had experienced the Civil War, Charles Leavell Moses was the first Congressman, but before that time, his father, Ansley Moses, was captain of the fifty-third Georgia Regiment, Company D, in the army of Northern Virginia. At first Ansley opposed Secession, but when Georgia seceded

Ansley joined. He became an officer because the men who farmed around him said, 'Hey Ansley, we'll follow you.' By the end of that year, he had been promoted to a Colonel fighting under Robert E. Lee. Ansley fought in all of General Lee's campaigns and was wounded and captured just south of Knoxville, Tennessee after the battle of Chickamauga. Ansley survived two more years in dismal conditions as a prisoner of war at Ft. Delaware, and was released at the end of the war.

"To get home, the Colonel had to walk from Delaware all the way back to Newnan, Georgia. Can you imagine? He dragged his buckshot-filled leg by propping himself up on his rifle that served as his crutch. By the time that he got home, he was crippled, and couldn't work the farm anymore. A black farm hand named Samuel, who was freed after Lincoln's Emancipation Proclamation, worked with Ansley and took Moses as his last name.

"Then, rather than sitting home feeling sorry for himself, Ansley started up a school for boys, to fulfill a promise to help Sam get a high school education. In turn, Sam worked the farm and helped provide food for the family. Sam was the first black man in Georgia to get a high school diploma, and he got it from our great-great-grandfather's school."

Marina could see the pride behind Tommy's words and knew that Charlie must've been equally proud. Mesmerized by his stories, she motioned to Tommy to continue.

"These kinds of stories from the lineage, coupled with historical events, show how tough our relatives were during tough times. They also held beliefs honed by their toughness.

One belief was that you don't pass money to the next generation. Doing so prevented the younger people's building of character, and character was more important than money.

"When our dad left mom, her family had already given the family money away. Uncle Luther Tellus Moses helped found and donated seventeen million dollars to Emory University. He left Grandpa his old Cadillac, but he left no money to mother. The thinking was you should make it on your own. If you don't do that, you will lack character. For instance, grandpa was eligible to pick up Social Security when it was new in the Roosevelt era, but he felt it was wrong because he never contributed to it. He said, 'I don't need Social Security. I didn't pay into it. I didn't earn it. Why should I take it? Taking something that is not yours is wrong.'

"Grandpa did have a pension of seven hundred and forty-four dollars a month from Bethlehem Steel. In those days, he could live on seven hundred and forty-four dollars a month. But he was fighting for every breath and dying from emphysema. Every month that he lived, he gave mother his seven hundred and forty-four dollars. For her, the money was the difference between putting food on the table and having to sell the house. Grandpa was a strong character, and my brother Charlie is like him, quite a strong character." ■

6. Teen Rebellion

"Opportunities don't happen. You create them."
—Chris Grosser

McCallie School for Boys had been a well-respected school since 1905. When Charlie was in ninth grade, the school's football coach moved him from his favorite position as quarterback to the linebacker position to make room for another quarterback. Though he was only in ninth grade, Charlie said that if he couldn't be the quarterback, then he would leave and do something else. He had sworn he would be at the "top of the heap." The coach's move made him feel disrespected.

He started smoking cigarettes publicly and explored smoking marijuana secretly. Somehow, he talked his mom into writing out a permission slip granting him permission to smoke cigarettes on campus. When the football coach, John Day, walked by the smoking youth, he shook his head in disapproval. Charlie became resentful and the feeling only became stronger. He substituted smoking cigarettes for going to church sometimes, causing his mother alarm and concern. Drinking alcohol at age fourteen made him more defiant, and the defiance soon extended to skipping church altogether. His new Sunday activity was to sit in a booth at the Waffle House across the street from the church and smoke cigarettes. Like most teens growing up the 1960s, he flirted with the idea of the Summer of Love happening in San Francisco. Charlie wanted to be part of the adventure, and instead he felt left behind. He started down the path of drugs and al-cohol because he was restless, irritable, and discontent. He walked away from church and religion and didn't want to par-ticipate in anymore Bible studies. His feelings of unaddressed abandonment issues from his parents' divorce got channeled into drinking alcohol and doing drugs, which masked the pain. However, in his rebellion, he became more popular with his peers.

One day, the school's headmaster called Charlie into his office to discipline him for bringing marijuana on campus. The headmaster asked, "Have you been selling marijuana on campus?"

"No, Dr. Spence, it's not like that. I've been giving it away."

Dr. Spence patiently explained, "Charlie, your family has a long, time-honored relationship at this school. Normal-ly an act like this would warrant immediate expulsion. But, considering your grandfather and father went here, and your uncle is on the Board of Directors, your punishment for this incident will be detention for six weeks."

"Sir, I politely refuse such a generous offer. Instead, I think now is the perfect time to part ways. I would rather go to public school."

The headmaster shook his head. The gesture seemed one of resignation, or even sadness. "Son, I'm sorry to hear that. I'm going to call your mother to come pick you up."

But Charlie replied, "I'll get home by myself," and he hitchhiked home.

The Third Brother, Chris

Chris was the third of the four boys. Being closer in age, Tommy and Charlie had developed a strong bond. By the time Chris came along, he was more of an independent child and only tagged along with them, if permitted. Tommy and Charlie had very strict rules for their areas of the basement rooms. Chris was never allowed to go near their stuff, and, at times, he was terrified of his brothers.

When he and Marina were the only two in the hospital room with Charlie, he took it upon himself to fill in the gaps where Tommy left off. "Growing up, we had been going to a Methodist church on Signal Mountain up to the time our parents divorced. I was six, Charlie was about eight, and Tommy was about ten. At that age, Tommy was involved with the Boy Scouts troop at church. After a while, mom shopped around and found a different church, and we started going to a church down in Chattanooga, but Tommy never went with us.

"He stayed at that church on Signal Mountain. I saw Tommy as self-driven. He had his personal faith, motivation, and values, and I didn't want to betray that. Tommy felt loyal to that church. We called Tommy "The Golden Boy" because of his strong directions and self-motivation.

"Charlie came along with mom, Ellis and me to church, until he could finally get mom to agree that he didn't have to go anymore. By the time Charlie was in junior high and high school, he was the black sheep of the family—he was the epitome of the hippy, liberal sixties child.

"I went to church on Wednesday nights and Sunday mornings with mom. On Sunday nights, I participated in the youth group at church. I grew up involved with the church. But, as an adult, I haven't had anything to do with the church." Chris described one truth that stands out about the four brothers, and it is reflected in how his brothers responded and showed up when Charlie was sick. Think of the old standard: I might fight with my brother, but if somebody else fights with my brother, I stand beside him.

"We do have a sense of loyalty, Chris said. "We may not always like each other, but we definitely love each other."

The Fourth Brother, Ellis

In childhood, Charlie once pointed out to Ellis his view of the brothers' birth order. Tommy was the king for a year and a half. Then Charlie was born and Tommy was dethroned. Charlie was dethroned a year and a half later when Chris came along. Then three-and-a-half years later, when Ellis was born, Charlie claimed Ellis as his baby because Ellis dethroned Chris.

The situation at home was not a good one. The boys' mom and dad were in a bad marriage and were about to get a divorce. On the way home from the hospital, mom was trying to figure out where they were going to put the new baby. Charlie said, "Put him in my room." Basically, Charlie took on baby Ellis as his project.

Ellis was also a tag-along to Chris. Chris and Ellis sat

around the house and played: checkers, chess, card games, and anything else they could create. They shot down standing cards with rubber bands or played other board games. Ellis and Chris seemed good friends as well as brothers; whereas, Tommy and Charlie were two athletically-inclined brothers who had grown up in competitive ways.

Ellis was the observer who knew where lines were drawn—both in the family and also in the community. He didn't feel the need to test the water and could stay away from trouble or never got caught because he watched Charlie when he was in trouble. The idea of being yelled at or getting arrested was far scarier for Ellis. On the exterior, he had the golden boy persona, although he was not a skilled athlete until he went to high school, and even then he felt that he never had Charlie's prowess.

Whenever there was an outside force or threat, the four brothers stuck together. If anyone insulted or accused one Gardner brother, or especially their mother, the brothers would stick together. One story Ellis shared over the years about Charlie, who was around age nine at the time, was when he was playing down the street from their house and he happened to be next to Anne Dooley, who was one of seven children who lived on the same street. Anne was trying to ride a bicycle and fell over. One Dooley assumed it was Charlie's fault that she fell over. Mr. Dooley, being sort of the town drunk, was an angry man that the neighborhood kids avoided. Now, he showed up with his two oldest boys at the door, threatening that they were going to teach Charlie Gardner a lesson.

Mom only opened the door as far as the chain allowed. Charlie and Tommy, who were standing behind their Mom, were aiming to defend their honor.

"Let us out, Mom. We can take them. We can show them!"

Instead, Mom threatened to take on Mr. Dooley herself, and the whole crisis subsided.

The Gardner brothers celebrated Tommy's naval career and his football prowess as he played linebacker for the Navy. They celebrated how well both Charlie and Chris have done in their careers. They rooted and cheered for one another, as well as grumbled or got pissed at times. What's good to know is that it never lasted too long. As Ellis has said time and time again, "We are fortunate that there doesn't seem to be bad blood between any of the four of us. All of the brothers are trained engineers who graduated from very good schools. All of us found employment, as mom was clear that each of us would have to make our own way."

Mom was an only child, and when their grandmother passed away in 1968, her father came to live with them. Then he passed away in 1972. Mother invested in two stocks and pretty much didn't touch those. She was smart enough to know to hold onto them for the rest of her life and then passed them to her sons. Well, the two companies she invested in were called Exxon and the Bell South (AT&T) Company. Then magic happened! The two stocks grew to be worth roughly eight hundred thousand dollars. She had been worried that her assets would not support her living in a senior center. As it was, she would have been absolutely fine for the rest of her life. ■

7. If You Want It, You Work for It!

As a young teen, Charlie maintained a good work ethic and never shied away from work. He cut grass in the summertime, saved the money he earned to buy a car, and got his learner's permit. He drove a few licensed buddies to school in his '56 Chevy.

On his 16th birthday, Charlie took five friends and drove out to the Tennessee State Highway Patrol Office. He took the written driver's test, and then went outside to meet the officer, who would ride with him for the driver's test. The officer was a big, tall, black highway patrolman with the wide-brim patrol hat. His size and authority commanded respect. Typical of Southern officers at the time, he chewed on a toothpick as he looked in Charlie's car. He nodded his head, acknowledging the five guys, who looked like they came straight off the movie set of American Graffiti. Two of them had a pack of cigarettes rolled up in their tee shirt sleeves. They tried to look tough.

The officer asked, "Boy, is that your vehicle?"

"Yes, sir." Charlie answered, perhaps wondering why he was being asked.

"How long you been driving?" the officer continued.

"Since I got my learner's permit, sir." Even Charlie knew when to be respectful.

"Those boys your friends." It was almost a statement

rather than a question.

"Most of 'em, sir," Charlie said, just to see what would happen.

"I don't need to take you on no driver's test. You go on. Get outta here!" After a student passed the written driver's exam, the officer had the option of going or not with Charlie for a test drive. Since Charlie had already been driving, the officer waived that test.

Charlie got in the driver's seat, and his friends encouraged him: "Peel out, peel out. I dare you to peel out." It was hilarious. It was fun. They were teenagers. Charlie peeled out, leaving rubber on the Amnicola Highway.

Going to California

Once Charlie had his driver's license, and as he steered away from church, he also stayed away from the house for several days at a time. He partied with his friends at places like the Blue Hole, The Rock, and George Hampton's abandoned house. Charlie listened to great music with both local talent and the fame seekers trying to make a name in Nashville. He was rebellious, and when he did return home one day, his desperate mom was on the phone with the police trying to find him.

Charlie told her to hang up the phone. "I'm okay. But, Mom, I've made the decision—I'm going to California." She hung up the phone. She was sad and looked at him with resignation. A moment of regret even passed through Charlie's heart that he was the cause of her distress.

Then she said, "Well, just make sure you stop and see your dad as you go through Memphis."

The regret passed quickly enough, and Charlie was on the road to California. He finally felt free and made it to Memphis with fifty-eight cents in his pocket. He made a smart move by taking his mother's advice and stopped to call his dad.

"Can you buy me a tank of gas?"

His dad responded to Charlie's call, bought gas, and then invited him to stay. "Charlie, I'll stay at my girl's house. You can have this house on two conditions. One, you've got to stay in school. Two, you've got to go to work." At age seventeen, Charlie thought those were great conditions.

Thus, Charlie didn't quite make it to California. He moved into his Dad's house and lived there for several years. Charlie enrolled in high school and got a permit to work. His first job was pumping gas at the Exxon station next to Graceland, Elvis's home. He worked his way up to night manager by putting in several hours of work in the afternoon and evening and going to school during the day.

The hippie movement was happening. Charlie, on the other hand, was a teenager in high school with a house he called his own. In his mind, maybe being in Memphis, Tennessee was way better than going west, especially when Dad's home became party central. He learned to juggle a social life with school and a working life. Since school wasn't high on Charlie's list of priorities at the time, his parents were both concerned. After some scrapes with the law, spiraling drug use, and wild parties at his house, his parents decided that the best thing for Charlie was to send him to a boarding school in Jacksonville, Florida. Knowing Charlie's stubborn streak, they bribed him, "If you go there to finish up your high school diploma, we'll buy you a Harley-Davidson motorcycle."

Although Charlie made it through school in Florida, the bike he got was a Norton 750 rather than a Harley. The Norton didn't run at the time, and that convinced his parents that he would be so busy fixing it that he would stay out of trouble. Hey, the bike could be an early graduation present! When his parents agreed, Charlie pushed the bike back to campus, and there it sat. In fact, Charlie never fixed it up and left it behind upon graduation.

Graduation from high school left Charlie with even more time to party, to be free, or to ride to California. But he did none of those things. Instead, he got a job working construction sites in Texas and Oklahoma.

Though he had become a laborer with real, honest work and decent pay while the company built hotels in the Midwest, Charlie watched and learned as the older workers struggled. He saw them on job sites trying to climb ladders, hoisting tools up to the higher floors. Wow! No way did he want to become some fifty-year-old guy still wearing a nail bag and trying to climb ladders. As much as he hated the discipline of school and homework, he thought he might need to go back to school. But how or when?

Developing Faith

At that age, Charlie didn't realize yet how God works in people's lives. However, one day the foreman fired him from the construction job. Once the company moved on to the next project, they didn't want him to continue on their payroll. Charlie called his mom, and she sent him the bus fare to get back to Tennessee. Free spirit that he was, though, Charlie had a better plan. He thought a greater adventure would be to hitchhike home to Tennessee.

In the meantime, Charlie's dad had moved to Little Rock, Arkansas. Charlie called him as he passed through: "Hey, Dad. I'm out here on the highway and hitchhiking. Just calling to say hello."

"Hi, Charlie. I'm getting ready to go to lunch with a business client. Do you want to have lunch together? I'll come and get you."

"Yeah, sure." Dad's lunch was with an engineer that he frequently called on for business. Dad was a manufacturers' representative for different types of instrumentation devices that go on wastewater treatment plants. During lunch, the engineer looked Charlie straight in the eye and asked, "What are you going to do?"

"Oh, I'm hitchhiking back to Tennessee. I just got let go at my construction job."

The engineer from Mehlburger Engineering in Little Rock, said, "We're looking for a few people on a survey crew that's going on down in Fort Polk, Louisiana. Would you be interested?"

"Sure, I'm looking for work."

He wasn't looking for a job, but work sure sounded better than going back to school. Thus, Charlie signed on with an engineering firm in Fort Polk, Louisiana, surveying officers' quarters for an addition to the Army base. The job involved pioneering new layouts through the swamps in the summer heat of the Louisiana Bayou. To combat illness, mosquitos, and other relentless insects, the construction crew was sprayed down with industrial strength insecticide and took Sulpher tablets. The tablets made the men smell like rotten eggs, which kept mosquitos away and leeches from attaching to their legs. On average, the crew killed six or more poisonous snakes a day, which was the daily routine when wading through the swamps of Louisiana.

Charlie liked the honest work because he had learned that ethic from his parents, especially his mother. But the labor aspect hardened him, and he caught a glimpse of how different the work world was from his previous experience. He had a chance to interface with the home office in Little Rock now and then, and he came to admire the professional men and women he met. They were all engineers, and most of them had graduated from the University of Arkansas.

Could he take this career path?

Charlie lobbied the executives in the Mehlburger Engineering Firm by presenting them with a plan to intern with the firm while he attended school. He could work when he was available and demonstrated that he had a real knack for the training in the world of engineering.

The firm felt Charlie had paid his dues and proved his

worth surveying in Louisiana, so they agreed to give him the opportunity to co-op or intern. He was on his way to become a professional engineer. The work was interesting to Charlie, as he then spent the summer processing blueprints from vellum copies. He performed an EPA Step 1 survey of existing sewer lines for a system upgrade plan, and learned the art of drafting.

Charlie was paying his way by now with only limited help from his parents, so he rented an apartment in Little Rock. He took introductory courses in geology, surveying, and basic engineering at the local community college in the hopes of shaping his future. The company started Charlie in their office the next summer, and he paid his way through college by working full-time during the summer and between semesters.

Charlie was now taking the responsible steps that lead to an engineering career that would be his life's work. He was on his way, and so close to a good career and future, but other things proved too tempting.

The Bud Man

Charlie needed to attend the University in Fayetteville, Arkansas to complete his engineering degree. His friends urged him to participate in fraternity life by saying "If you go up to Fayetteville, you need to join a fraternity. The town of Fayetteville is a small town, and the Greek system is strong. We are all Pikes (Pi Kappa Alpha), and you should join, too."

Fraternities were recruiting Charlie, and initially he resisted, protesting, "No, I'm not that kind of person, I don't want to be like a robot, you know. Everybody wears the same clothes, looks and acts the same, and must conform. Not interested!"

"No, no. It's not like that, Charlie," people insisted. "The fraternity that we belong to has cool guys. Really! There are only two choices. You're in a fraternity because it's an active Greek system. We get all the pretty girls, and we party all the time. You have to join a fraternity, or else you're stuck with all the geeks in the dorm."

Well, that made the decision easy. Charlie decided he'd rather be a Greek than a geek.

Charlie joined Pi Kappa Alpha and began his studies at the University of Arkansas. Having been out of school while he was working for a few years, his life now became work hard and party hard. Most of the fraternity brothers were eighteen and nineteen years old. Charlie was twenty-one, which meant he could buy the booze. The fraternity brothers also elected him as the pledge class president because they reasoned, "He was older and more mature." Sure!

The problem was, Charlie was one of those guys who fit the typical pattern of an alcoholic. Two main characteristics of an alcoholics is that they have a big ego, but low self-esteem. Charlie wanted to be the number one guy, and he had always been this way. If he couldn't be the best in something, he lost interest and left to do something else. This made Charlie a natural as president of the pledge class.

All the pledges completed their first semester, then

went through hell week, and finally became fraternity members. It was then when the pledge class elected Charlie to be the Special Projects Chairman.

"And just what does that duty entail?" Charlie asked the fraternity president.

"Well, you're the guy who organizes our fundraisers to give money to the local charities. It's all for us to improve our public relations."

"That's cool. What does the frat normally do?"

"Well, we take coffee cans and stand around on street corners and collect donations."

"Really? For real? "

"Yeah!"

"So, we beg for it?"

"Yeah. How else are we going to get it?"

"No, we're not going to do that. We're going to do something big. We need the best."

In the meantime, Charlie was dating Kay Ratcliff from Lubbock, Texas. She invited Charlie to go home with her to Lubbock for spring break. The underlying message was "come with me to meet my parents." On the drive to Lubbock, Kay said, "You know, my sorority and your fraternity are having a social on Tuesday or Wednesday night. We can go to that because you're a member of that fraternity."

"Tell me more about it," Charlie said as they drove.

"The fraternity, Pi Kappa Alpha, is having a huge party that includes every fraternity and every sorority from Texas Tech University. The sororities sell food, and the fraternities play games. They have live bands, and we go through about three hundred kegs of beer over the weekend. It's a big party. We do it Texas style."

Of course, Charlie couldn't wait to attend this huge, free party with Kay. For three days, he drank beer and stumbled around in amazement, saying, "These guys have got it going on. What a great idea! I'm going to take this back to my fraternity, and we'll do that to raise money to give to charity. We're going to do Pike-Fest at the University. That's how we'll get our publicity."

The fraternity members applauded Charlie's idea and were ready to get the project underway. Several fraternity brothers said that Charlie should talk to the local Budweiser distributor, who could probably give the fraternity a good deal on beer since he was fraternity alum. The distributor heard Charlie's pitch, and took it to the next level, "You know, we're looking for a sharp guy like you. I just got back from St. Louis. The company is looking for a man like you to help us roll out this marketing program called the 'Bud Man on Campus.' B-M-O-C. Get it? Instead of the Big Man on Campus, you could be the Bud Man on Campus. In fact, I'd like you to be that man."

Perhaps several years earlier, Charlie would have jumped on board without much thought. This time, he backed away, reasoning: "No, I can't do that. I'm a sophomore in civil engineering. I'm taking eighteen hours. I'm totally busy."

However, the Bud Man shared a different scenario. "Well, let me just tell you what the deal would be. Then decide. We will pay for all your books and tuition. I'll give you five hundred dollars a week in cash, and a dollar for every keg you sell, and seventy-five cents for every case of beer you sell. We'll put your name and picture in the student newspaper. You'll be famous. We've got this dune buggy out back that you can drive around campus. Think of it! Here comes the Bud Man."

"You know, it all sounds great, but I really can't." Thoughts of all the responsibilities he'd have to juggle raced around in his mind.

"Are you sure?" the man pressed. "You can use my Lincoln Continental or my Suburban with notice. You'll call on all the fraternities and sororities, and you will be famous, and everybody on campus will know who you are. Not only that, you'll never have to buy a drink for the rest of the time you're in college."

Charlie tried to resist, but the excitement was building with each extra bonus the distributor mentioned. It was all very compelling, and Charlie's hand shot up. "Okay. Yes, I'm your guy!"

"Yes!" You won't regret it, no one ever has.

The Bud distributor walked Charlie to the hangar-sized warehouse where cases of beer covered the walls, wall-to-wall. They walked into the cooler where kegs of beer stacked from the floor to the ceiling, Charlie felt like the character Norm on the TV show "Cheers" and said, "I'm Home!"

They put his picture and name in the college student newspaper: Charlie Gardner, your Bud Man on Campus. Ready to service your party needs, large or small!

For the next seven years (yes, seven) that it took Charlie to get through college, he was the Bud Man on campus.

With each passing year, the age gap grew—the students were getting younger, and Charlie was growing older. Wherever he went, especially a bar or a restaurant, someone yelled, "The Bud Man's here!" Charlie's ego grew along with his fame. If his head really could swell with so much attention, it would have gotten to the point where he practically had to turn sideways to get through the door. The Bud Man bought rounds for the whole house, and all he had to do was sign for it. He was a drunk in the making with the role he now played.

**Charlie as a college student
with two friends drinking.**

In addition, the Bud folks came to his residence, which was an off-campus house, and fixed it up because the Bud Man needed to have a first class, top-shelf bar, a pool room, billiards, and darts. Every Tuesday like clockwork, the Bud folks changed out the kegs at his house. He had to have fresh beer to serve because he was constantly inviting people over and scheduling social events. The Bud Man was secretly initiated into four different fraternities, as well as several sororities because he handled their parties. The fraternity brothers and sorority sisters got drunk, and each invited Charlie to join by offering him an honorary membership. Having that keg in his house probably cost him at least two extra semesters in calculus. Trying to do calculus with a cold beer sitting right next to him was nearly impossible.

The role of Bud Man continued between Charlie's twenty-first to his twenty-sixth years, when he was finally on track to graduate and move forward. However, Charlie had devised several promotions that were picked up nationally by Anheuser-Busch. They put him on the list of the top-ten campus beer representatives dubbed the "Brew Crew."

Charlie went to St. Louis twice a year to attend the Think Tanks, which in effect were weekend drunks. Their purpose was to discuss which promotions were working on college campuses and why so they could replicate it where others were failing. Charlie often heard, "Hey, that kid from Arkansas has a great idea. We're taking that national." For years, the Marketing Director of Anheuser-Busch would call Charlie to bounce off the latest marketing ideas and get feedback, since his ideas were so spot on and tuned into college life.

Early Career

Finally, though, Charlie graduated and started sending resumes to engineering firms. He went through what he described as senior shock. The University trained him to be a design engineer. Most of the people graduating from the Civil Engineering program went to the Gulf of Mexico and worked on offshore platforms owned by Gulf Oil, Texaco, or another Texas company. In his mind, he didn't want to be that dumb SOB that acted like he knew it all but was too inexperienced to match up with veteran professionals.

However, he had an offer from Anheuser-Busch to be the Assistant Beer Brand Manager for Michelob Lite. He was so instrumental in helping to promote their counter Miller Lite, Busch, and Michelob Light, that they offered him a job. As it turned out, the key guys that had supported Miller Lite's "Taste Great – Less Filling" campaign recently left Anheuser-Busch. Charlie pointed out during a Brew Crew meeting that management was remiss in letting these guys go, as they had their "finger on the pulse" of what is going on with the American youth. He was put down, like what does this kid from Arkansas know?

At the same time, Brinderson Corporation of Irvine, California, offered Charlie a job as an assistant project engineer at a wastewater treatment plant in Atlanta, Georgia. When he started school, the going rate for civil engineers was ten thousand dollars a year, and that was a lot of money at the time. When he finished school seven years later, the going salary was twenty thousand dollars a year.

The offer from Anheuser-Busch to be this assistant

beer brand manager meant flying around on a corporate Lear jet and earning forty-four thousand dollars a year–more than twice as much as the construction company offered. However, Charlie turned Anheuser-Busch down, and took the job as an engineer at the wastewater treatment plant because in the end, he didn't want to end up a washed-up alcoholic loading kegs of Pabst Blue Ribbon in Detroit, Michigan.

This was Charlie's first inkling that maybe he was having a problem with the booze. He watched himself do inappropriate things like getting drunk at parties and making advances toward other friends' girlfriends.

Charlie didn't feel that he would be a good role model as the representative of Anheuser-Busch on campus. He would wash out, which he heard a happened a lot to flash-in-the-pan Anheuser-Busch salespeople.

Instead, he was working, and on his way up at this waste water plant in Atlanta, Georgia. Another Brew Crew member from New York took the position as assistant beer brand manager. He took great delight in calling Charlie every so often.

"Hey Charlie, what are you doing?"

"I'm checking rebar drawings on this crap plant in Atlanta, Georgia. What are you doing?"

"Oh, I'm flying in the corporate Lear jet out to this annual ski event we sponsor for Michelob Light in Aspen. I'm here with Monique St. Pierre, who was the Playmate of the year nineteen-eighty-four. Say hello to Monique, Charlie."

Charlie resented the calls and cursed as he slammed the phone down. But he kept his nose to the grindstone and followed his work ethic hard and still partied hard. Charlie socialized in Atlanta's night life, and his hedonistic lifestyle did not include church, or God, or a spiritual path. He worked his way up to project engineer because his performance was so good and the company eventually transferred him to Ft. Lauderdale to help run a treatment plant there.

Could Love Last?

By now Charlie was engaged to Shirley Gardner, a woman he met during college registration when he was twenty-two years old. They shared the same last name, which seemed prophetic at the time, and dated on and off from their sophomore year through college. Charlie stayed faithful to her despite the fact he could have had practically any girl he wanted. After all, he drove the Bud Man buggy around campus, and girls ran out of their sorority houses calling, "Chas, Chas, take us promoting." And he did. Shirley would wisely comment that she had seen him promoting around campus, but trusted his fidelity since she loved him as much as he loved her.

Charlie proposed to Shirley when he was graduating, and she had one year left before her graduation. However, when he transferred and got promoted to go to Ft. Lauderdale, Shirley said, "I thought we were going to move to San Francisco to be near my parents. You promised me that."

Yes, he had promised her they would live in San Francisco, but at the time, he was younger and more selfish. He told her, "We have to follow my career since I'm the one making money. When you get out of school, if you have a job that's making more money, then we'll pursue your career. I promise you, after Ft. Lauderdale, I'll come to California, maybe to Southern California first since the company is there." After that conversation, rightfully, she lost trust in him. She was hurt and reminded Charlie of his previous promises. "How do I know you're not going to get some bigger job and move to New York?" She called off the engagement. Charlie was crushed, and what did he do when he felt crushed? His answer was to drink more and party more and mostly to forget not being chosen.

Sex, Drugs, and Rock n' Roll

Just shy of thirty years old and in the mid-1980's, Charlie now lived and worked in Ft. Lauderdale. This was also during the time of the cocaine wars in Florida. From his job working at the George T. Lohmeyer Wastewater Treatment Plant right by Pier 66, Charlie watched merchant marines park their boats at the piers. They didn't check through customs, but instead they walked right through the buildings carrying big duffle bags, ostensibly to wash their laundry. But they were laundering other things in this wild southern paradise.

Charlie finally felt like he belonged. He earned a top salary, lived in a beautiful setting, and had a favorite bar on the Inter-Coastal Waterway. One time, the bartender addressed Charlie, "You know, I've been watching you. I'm not gay or anything, but I know you from somewhere."

Charlie looked at the bartender and soon realized that he grew up with this man, Jimmy Vann, on Signal Mountain. "Yeah, I remember you. We grew up together. I remember you had that hot little sister named Betsy. Where's she at?"

"Oh, she'll be in town today from Modesto, California. She's just getting divorced, but she'll be at the here at the bar tomorrow. Why don't we all hook up and party and remember old times?"

They did hook up. Charlie immediately started dating Jimmy's sister Betsy while she was in Florida. He went straight from being crushed in a romantic relationship to embracing the party life again. The reality was this: The cocaine poured into Fort Lauderdale. Big bales of marijuana, chased by gun runners, washed up on the shore. As Charlie drove to and from work on the main highway, some people often hung out of their car windows, shooting Uzi machine guns at each other. It was right where he wanted to be at the time!■

8. Young Man Goes West

"Go West Young Man, and grow up with the country".
—John Babsone Lane Soule 1851

As much as Florida seemed like a kind of Wild West at the time, Charlie got promoted to senior estimator and was told he would actually be moving west—he would be working at the home office in Irvine, California. He left the crazy life of Florida behind and landed in Dana Point, California, which was a beautiful area in Southern Orange County that hugged the Pacific coastline.

When Charlie moved to Dana Point, one of the first people he met was Roger Berry, who worked locally at Harpoon Henry's Seafood Restaurant. After work, Charlie visited with Roger, had a beer and a shot, then relished the smoked fish for dinner. Over time, he drank more hard liquor and got drunk more often, yet somehow Charlie usually made it home before he passed out.

Roger and Charlie became best friends and roommates, along with Tom Hanley and Bill Basset, who also worked at Harpoon Henry's. Charlie, Roger, and Tom, close friends who called each other the Three Muskateers, were roommates when Tom met Lisa. Lisa became part of the gatherings after work, where they played cards, drank, did drugs, and partied. Of the group, Lisa often described Charlie as the financially responsible one, Roger was the fun one, and Tom was the organized one.

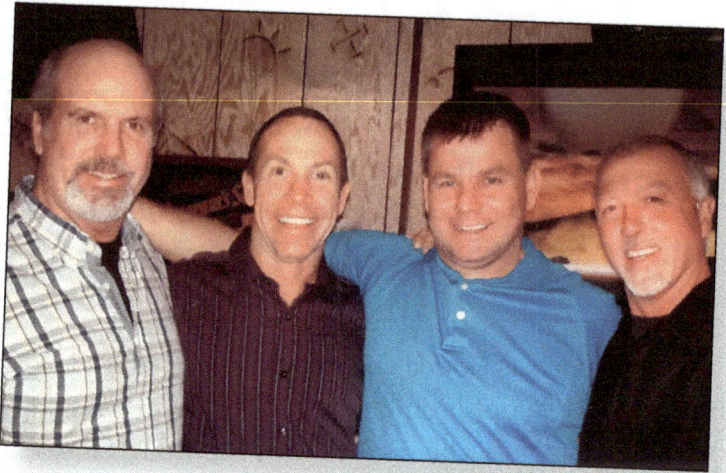

Charlie, Bill Bassett, Roger Berry, and Tom Hanley ■

Lisa and Tom were a couple when they moved from Dana Point to the San Francisco Bay area. Charlie lived with Tom and Lisa several times over the years when he started a new job, visited the area, or was getting sober. The couple were with Charlie when he made some hard life transitions, but that didn't stop such good friends from traveling together to Costa Rica, as well as to several cruises to Italy and Greece.

In the earlier days of the Three Musketeers, Roger organized poker party nights at the house to make rent money from all the restaurant's bartenders and waitresses, who came to the party. Charlie enjoyed the party life while also working hard to fill his job's expectations. Some episodes of partying interfered with work, yet his mind always churned with project ideas and planning. At four o'clock one morning, as the party was still happening, Charlie unrolled a set of plans on the kitchen table in the midst of the melee to determine his bid for an upcoming project. Life in the 1980s was working hard, partying hard, drinking hard, doing drugs, and having relationships.

Two men, with whom Charlie worked on the Atlanta job site, recruited him to his first job as a project manager in 1989. He was charged with running a small waste water treatment plant in Fort AP Hill, Virginia. He worked out of the Richmond office. This upgrade of the Army Base was in preparation for the National Boy Scout Jamboree. Charlie moved to Virginia to run this job and hired Roger as an assistant office engineer.

Roger and Charlie found an old Victorian home sitting on eighty acres of what used to be an old Civil War battlefield near Spotsylvania, Virginia. The house was available because it was rumored to be haunted. That didn't matter to Roger or Charlie.

The Dog Knows

Charlie had a German Shepherd puppy at the time. They were concerned about her following the long driveway out of the house down to the main road. At the same time, they also started hearing noises around the house. Their first thought was that it had to be the rumored ghosts. Then one morning when Charlie went to the bathroom, he found Civil War relics in the toilet. They might have been the uniform buttons of soldiers from both the North and the South, or they might have been bullets. That the house was haunted in weird and freaky ways made Charlie even more determined to get to the bottom of the situation.

Then it happened! Charlie heard noises in the bathroom one night. He quietly crept his way to a confrontation in the bathroom. But what if there was a ghost? Of course, he couldn't think about that prospect.

He popped the door open and turned on the light—only to find the German Shepherd pup drinking out of the toilet. Charlie would never know if that smart dog dropped the relics in there deliberately. What he did know was that she would dig around the expansive property, collect her findings in her mouth, then come back inside and drink from the toilet. Buttons and bullets clanged against porcelain as they dropped to the bottom of the toilet bowl. Mystery solved!

As Charlie and Roger completed their first project, the Norfolk Corps of Engineers recommended them for a meritorious award—one of only two awarded since 1880. But then the company reneged on their bonus pay because the two were already making a lot of money. When they explained that Charlie's deal would require them to pay more than they were willing to pay, Charlie quit. He returned to California and went to work on a major waste-water treatment plant called Hyperion, named for one of the twelve Titans in Greek mythology, in El Segundo, California near Manhattan Beach and Hermosa Beach.

Despite all of his successes, Charlie was still often drinking to get drunk and had become enamored with cocaine. Yet he could stay up all night and still make it to work and get the job done the next day. However, when the owner of Hyperion passed away, and the company folded, Charlie decided he would like to live in Northern California. He landed his next job by calling several contacts. After this cold-calling, Charlie had two opportunities available. One company, Kiewit, was building segments of the I-280 freeway. The other company had a treatment plant in Gilroy, California.

Charlie took the job building the treatment plant in Gilroy, as it could have been a high point as a senior project manager. The company promised bonuses, promotions, and a raise. However, they moved him to a lateral position and said, "Gee, we didn't do well this year. Sorry, there are no bonuses." Charlie had suspected as much and already had a backup plan. He relocated once more to Southern California and became a vice president of operations, where he would go on to earn well over six figures.

Memories of being the Bud Man weren't lost in this role. As VP of operations, Charlie had a nice company car and an expense account, got to meet Hollywood stars and attended private parties. And once again, the Bud Man, who was now approaching forty years of age, was continuing with the alcohol, cocaine, and other drug use. The lifestyle continued for another year and a half, and having hit rock bottom once, Charlie knew now that at forty, his body and brain could maintain drug habits for just so long before crashing. He would stop and buy at various liquor stores because the store clerk would not know his consumption levels. He kept telling himself, "I can't keep doing this. This is going to kill me." But his response to himself was always, "I will do something about it tomorrow though."

For years, Charlie's sobriety date was tomorrow.

Eventually, this decision cost Charlie. The president of the company called Charlie into his office and said, "Look we've made a decision. We're going to close your division." Charlie knew that the formal language meant, "We're firing you because...you are an alcoholic, you're not coming to work." The president continued, "We think you have a problem with alcohol, Charlie, and you should probably get some help."

At that time, Charlie was again with little money. His high income had been spent on his high lifestyle. After losing his job, he was evicted from his house because he couldn't pay rent.

Well, for Charlie, the time was now or never—it was his jumping-off point.

Charlie was truly blessed to have friends and family who had returned to sobriety before him. His buddy Roger had gone through recovery five years earlier and had planted the seed in Charlie's mind, telling him, "If you ever get to a place where you have nowhere to go, give me a call." Charlie was at that point: no job, no home, and no money. It was as if Roger had known.

Charlie's mother who cared and still worried about him called, "Come back to Tennessee, Charlie. You need help like I got for myself. You hit rock bottom. Charlie, please come home." Mom had gotten sober and explained how they came from a long line of alcoholics. His alcoholic grandfather drank himself out of a good job and tried to get sober in his late forties, the same age Charlie was heading for. He held recovery meetings in his home in Atlanta, Georgia. Mom looked through the stairway banister at the men smoking cigars and having their meeting. In the meantime, the women were in the kitchen at the back of the house baking cake or cookies, and brewing pots of black coffee. After the meeting, Charlie's grandfather didn't stay sober, and he asked Charlie, then a teenager, to go and buy booze. A request made because Mom had cut off his ability to call the drugstore and have the liquor delivered to his home.

Charlie viewed his Mom as an indomitable Southern lady, whom he greatly respected. He just couldn't go back to Tennessee. Pride got in his way.

God was gone, and Charlie had no place to live. Nowhere to go. So, he finally called his buddy Roger and said the magic words, "Roger, I need help."

"Where are you, Charlie?"

"I'm in Burbank."

"Okay, then get to the airport, Charlie. Get on a plane, and come here to Phoenix."

"Okay."

"Charlie, don't do anything else. Please, get to the airport and get here." Charlie knew the jig was up. Like a recalcitrant child, Charlie drank all the way to Phoenix and Roger picked him up at the airport. Roger asked, "So Charlie, when's the last time you had a drink?"

"On the plane, man." He couldn't help but be honest. Roger knew him so well.

Roger accompanied Charlie to his first recovery meeting, where a Max G. from Fresno, was speaking. Max G. appeared to be a tough, biker guy who garnered Charlie's attention. Max was one of those guys who decided to commit the ultimate sacrifice. Some years past, he had turned a shotgun toward his head and tried to blow his face off.

However, Max had survived. He had no eyes and no nose. A small hole was in place of his mouth. Charlie was compelled as he listened to Max as he was talking about surrender, and what it could do to a man. He commanded Charlie's utter attention. That meeting was Charlie's turning point of getting sober.

The irony was that Charlie's family grew up seventy miles from the dry county of Lynchburg, Tennessee, where they bottled Jack Daniels bourbon. Over the back side of Signal Mountain was Dayton, Tennessee, site of the Scopes Monkey Trial. This 1925 trial pitted Clarence Darrow, whose client was being prosecuted for teaching evolution in a public school, against the legendary William Jennings Bryan, who died immediately after the trial. To the north of Signal Mountain was Oakridge in Cleveland, Tennessee, the birthplace of the atomic bomb. Evolution or creationism? A-bomb or peacenik? Redneck or hippie? Bud Man or engineer? Wet or dry? Small wonder that Charlie's life was a confusing one. Even less surprising that he was now ready to surrender.

Charlie grew up in an era where he was a redneck, and a hippy, who dreamed of a metaphoric endless summer of love. He had also been confused, and now he was ready to surrender.

Self-Worth

Looking back to the years as Bud Man, Charlie could see that his self-worth was always wrapped up in his jobs, at which he had predictably been top-notch—when not drinking. However, he had not been successful in relationships. He was a good-looking guy and didn't have trouble attracting women, and he always seemed to attract the prettiest ones around. Perhaps he got bored too easily, tried too hard, or was simply too much a perfectionist. Maybe it was because he moved so often until he got sober.

He was a kind, good-hearted, happy drunk, which didn't matter much when his health started to fail at age 40 because of whiskey and cocaine abuse. Charlie had both stomach and intestinal problems. Sometimes, his esophagus closed and he couldn't swallow anything. While he told his friends that he had stomach problems, his physical problems were more typical of an alcoholic. His organs were melting. He had pancreatitis, which is when the pancreas releases so many enzymes for digestion that the enzymes start digesting the organ itself. His doctor's diagnosis also confirmed cirrhosis of the liver and Hepatitis C.

What the Gardner brothers' childhoods had in common was that a concerned single mom with a strong will raised four brothers. Their Mom was tied to God, thus they sat in the front row at the church, which in her mind meant that they had to pay attention. After all, the preacher was right in front of them. She groomed them to appreciate religion. On the other hand, their family line included that alcoholic gene, which made them more likely to develop the disease of alcoholism. Of course, environments factor in there also.

At that time, Ellis was a traveling salesman and not a realtor yet. He flew to Los Angeles to help Charlie pack up, and more than anything else, make sure he got on the plane. "We returned to Tennessee. His two dogs came with us and stayed in my fenced back yard," Ellis told Marina one afternoon at the hospital. "He applied to rehab here in Tennessee, but he didn't last a day. He decided 12-Step meetings were his path. So, I went with Charlie to a recovery meeting around Los Angeles when he realized that he needed to stop drinking. During the break, people broke out and everyone was smoking cigarettes, including Charlie and me.

"A man standing next to me asked, 'Where ya from?'

'Well, I think I'm from an alcoholic family.' Ellis let out a short laugh, but his heart wasn't laughing. He knew the toll alcohol had taken on the family.

"The conversation revealed that our grandfathers, both grandfathers, were alcoholics and stopped drinking late in their lives. Tommy remembers seeing Grandpa Moses, who lived with us at the time, drinking Aqua Velva in the morning. Grandpa was an old country boy, who could get alcohol from just about anything they could figure out. The local pharmacy that brought him his medicine also brought him toiletries, two gallons of Aqua Velva. That was his alcohol. Our mother soon cut off those deliveries, and she had no intention of letting him know where she hid her bottle of Jack Daniels.

"Tommy made the decision in high school that he was not going to drink, and he never has. Chris followed suit, but

Charlie gave in after that." Ellis put his head down in his hands and glanced up at his now comatose brother laying under hospital sheets. He finally looked back up at Marina, who had sat there quietly, and continued.

"Being fired from his job for the apparent alcoholism and being evicted from his home were the lowest blows in Charlie's life. He had emotional issues. He had no money and no credit. He went from making over six figures, living the cool lifestyle behind a facade to implosion. Despite feeling he was below the lowest point in his entire life, he couldn't know yet the plan that God had for him. He was yet to learn how resilient he could be. He would understand later that through his suffering and embarrassment, he would learn to help others, as others had helped him. His heart would heal when touched by the hand of God." Ellis grew quiet after his words, and he and Marina sat quietly by Charlie's side for the rest of the afternoon.

Finding Support

Returning to the Bay area brought to Charlie a fresh start. His good friends Tom and Lisa Hanley, had married and now lived in Berkeley. They said, "Charlie, come out and stay with us. You can look for a job here and go to recovery meetings in Berkley."

Charlie was busy looking for work, and landed a job with the firm Tutor-Saliba, who hired him as the project manager building the new rental car facility at San Francisco International Airport. Suddenly he had a new job and wanted to move to the coast. Unfortunately, he could find no rental property in the coastal area. Finally, he turned to a realtor who said, "Charlie, why don't you buy a place. Have a real home in this beautiful area, especially if you feel you want to stay awhile."

"Oh no, I can't buy a place. I have no credit. I don't have any money."

That statement didn't faze the realtor at all, who just told him, "Charlie, maybe I can find you a property that you can negotiate a lease option or something like that. You can get in and rent until you're on your feet again and can buy your home."

This time, Charlie turned the process over to God.

The realtor did indeed find a home for him. Miraculously, he then got a loan and bought the house with no money down. After closing on his home, he had $417 in the bank and he was going to trust God to help him make his first mortgage payment. Brother Tommy chastised Charlie for how much he was paying for this beachside house in Montara. "You're paying $280K for this place? Do you know what you can get in Tennessee for this amount of money!? What do you want it to go to, $500K? Charlie thought, "that would be nice".

Charlie was also in a recovery program to sustain his sobriety. The group members said, "Charlie, you need to find a power greater than yourself, a higher power. That's essential so you'll find strength and not return to your drug of choice."

Charlie reacquainted himself with the God of his childhood, the God of Abraham, Isaac, and Jacob. His simple prayer became, "God, help me."

In time, life was going well again. He had a house and a job. At 90 days sober, he rationalized that maybe it was the Scotch and the cocaine that were the problems. He told people, "I've never had trouble with beer and pot". So, he started to smoke a few joints. Of course, this backfired too. Charlie had been on the job for only about three weeks when an engineer approached him.

"Hey Charlie, have you taken your drug test yet?

"Uh, no, not yet."

"Oh, you should. Our boss is adamant about that. He hates drugs."

"Okay. Well, I can't do it now because I've got to go and see a realtor. I can do it Monday."

Charlie left the job site and freaked out while driving around Pacifica. "Oh, my God, what am I going to do? What am I going to do? What am I going to do?" The thoughts tumbled around and around in his head. While his thoughts were running on, he had a realization.

He could attend the recovery meeting in Pacifica, and it turned out to be the both the worst, and also the best, meeting he ever attended. A group of aging ladies talked about how they didn't have any toys when they were kids, and how their dads didn't love them. The conversation was irritating as well as devoid of any guidance that could help him figure out how to go through life sober. He wanted to get out of there as quickly as possible, but he couldn't physically leave. He really wanted to. He was trying, but he couldn't leave. As the group started the Lord's Prayer, Charlie felt the hand of God on his hand. He heard, "Stay right where you are, don't go."

The Lord's Prayer was over, and he was out the door, only then he heard a human voice behind him. "So, you wanted to leave this meeting, didn't you?"

Charlie turned around to face the calmer man and said, "Yeah, I've gone to this kind of meeting probably a thousand times, and this one was the worst one I've attended."

"Really?"

The man, John Gale, introduced himself to Charlie. Two hours later, both men were sitting in the parking lot. John told Charlie, "Maybe you need to lose this job and start to get serious about recovery. You know this disease kills people. Maybe you need to lose everything and get beat down to get serious about getting sober."

"Yeah, but you don't understand. This job is everything. I need this job." (This is what is called the "Yeah buts!")

"Well, maybe you need to lose that job instead of using yeah-buts."

"There's a meeting tonight at Half Moon Bay. I'll go to that."

"Okay. I've got an appointment, but maybe I can meet you." After the meeting at Half Moon Bay, the two men continued to talk in the parking lot afterward. Charlie asked, "I heard a lot about this deal called sponsorship. I need a sponsor. Would you be my sponsor?"

"Yeah. I'd be glad too. Now here's what I'd like you to do. I want you to go in Monday morning and take the drug test. No matter what the results may be, you are going to be okay. If you get fired, you're going to be fine. Just don't drink and don't use."

The premise of the conversation was that Charlie had to be willing to let go entirely and have faith and trust that whatever happened would be okay. Charlie turned the corner. He took the drug test, and for two weeks was sitting on pins and needles. He was on edge while waiting for a knock on the door, as if it would signal the end of his job.

Two weeks passed. There was no knock on the door.

The third week passed. Charlie was happy. He got by, and he still had the beer in the refrigerator and a joint to light. He went down to the beach and was about to light up when he heard, "No. You can't do that." He recoiled as if from a hot flame and flung the joint into the ocean.

The date was May 19, 1997. Charlie's authentic journey of sobriety began. Charlie, with his first sponsor, John Gale, worked the 12-Steps with a passion because Charlie was on fire. He couldn't get enough. How amazing it was when his head was clear of fog and drunkenness. He could see clearly that his life had taken on a whole new meaning with new inspiration.

The Time of His Life

Charlie's dreams were starting to come true. When Charlie first got into recovery, John advised him to make a list of what he truly wanted from life. He said, "Charlie, you want to write down ten things you want to come true in your life. Think outside the box. It can be anything you like, and go big - whatever dreams you want to come true and those miracles you want to have happen. Write down ten big things."

Of course, the big dreams Charlie thought about in early recovery were standard for recovery.

Charlie's list included:

Make a million dollars
Buy a house around Lake Tahoe
Get married
Have a beautiful honeymoon in the South Pacific

Charlie remembered his love for hiking, fishing, and admiring the sheer beauty of the Signal Mountain geography. When Charlie wanted to clear his mind, and find serenity in this chaotic life, he had his personal mind trick. He imagined the scene where he was on a fishing boat in the middle of the lake at 4:30 am, in the calm predawn. The lake was crystal clear with a flat, smooth surface, and the morning was quiet. Even the ducks skimmed the water so smoothly and silently as to leave barely a ripple. Life was good. Charlie was calm. Then, the big mouth bass sucked a big hole out of the water, and Charlie could yell, "Fish on."

During a visit to his mom, Charlie relished the memory as he talked to the pastor of the church he attended as a child. When the conversation led to Charlie's teen behavior,

he asked the pastor a simple question, "How can I find redemption? How can I be forgiven for all the bad things that
I've done throughout my life?"

The pastor replied, "Do you know the guy, David, who
killed the giant, Goliath? He wasn't a good guy either. Yes, he
became King of Israel, but he was also an adulterer and a
murderer. He did all kinds of bad things, and yet he was loved
by God. God loved him. David was the one who wrote the
Psalms. He wrote the prayers for forgiveness, and he was an
inspiration to his country. Although he did all these bad and
terrible things, he found redemption. Charlie, the recovery
program can help you find your redemption."

As Charlie worked through the steps over the next six
months, he found the pastor's statement to be true. One man
in the group asked Charlie to sponsor him. In discussing the
possibility with his sponsor, the best advice to Charlie was,
"You can help him along the way, but only as far as you have
come." He had to work harder to stay ahead of his new pro-
tege, which was a good thing.

When the student is ready, the teacher appears. The
first man whom Charlie sponsored was gay, forcing Charlie
to face the age-old prejudices from his Southern upbringing. Through him, Charlie learned how to be tolerant. He was
taught Christian values in childhood and felt like he had run
away from them in the past several years. Now, he was re-
learning and practicing the reality of living authentically. Charlie started to sponsor more men and became more active in
service. His sponsor explained that usually people with five or
more years of sobriety have some form of service because

that's essential to maintaining sobriety.

Charlie knew no one could think his way into sobriety or into becoming a better person. When he sponsored someone, saw the light come alive in their eyes, and watched delighted family members, Charlie knew that he had a small part in making it happen. Positive self-worth grew from these deeds.

The Yosemite Conference

Charlie was six months sober when Roger Berry asked him to go with him to a conference in Yosemite National Park. On that Saturday afternoon, Charlie and Roger took a hike to enjoy nature's beauty. They met a Canadian named Jim, who was traveling throughout the United States, attending recovery meetings, and was taking a year off to connect with others.

Roger, Charlie, and Jim had their own small meeting at Mirror Lake in Yosemite Park during a 12-Step recovery conference. At the end, they knelt to recite the Third Step Prayer. Charlie felt like he floated above the ground, electrified and attuned with his higher power. The other men appeared to have spiritual experiences also. They agreed to return the next year. Each year on the same day Charlie would return and host the Mirror Lake meeting. One year the meeting almost died when the sponsors of the conference refused to announce the Mirror Lake meeting because it "wasn't part of the conference." This caused Charlie to have resentment, and he walked through the cold freezing rain that year promising this was the last year he was going to do this meeting.

Then the miracle of recovery happened. Eight people had come through slushy rain to attend this session. The discussion focused on their recovery process through the last year. A young woman, perhaps in her twenties, stood up to share, "I'm so glad you guys have this gathering. I've been looking forward to this meeting for six months now. This year was great. I got engaged to be married. I was happy. I was in love. But my fiance committed suicide. His tragedy made me want to kill myself. I planned to join him in the ultimate sacrifice, and I had it all planned. I filled the tub and lit the candles. I closed the door to my bathroom, and there was a poster of Mirror Lake on the back of the door. I thought if I could just make it back to this meeting, I might have a chance."

She expressed the fact that she was extremely grateful, and that this meeting had literally saved her life. There was not a dry eye at that meeting, and after the Third Step Prayer was done, Charlie left that meeting with a renewed determination that he would continue to host that meeting going forward!

The meetings in Yosemite are still going on today because they are important in people's lives and nurturing to people's souls. The power of one young women's story or an older man's commitment to recovery proves that our passions are not distinct, nor our life journeys so different. When you have 250 people offering the Third Step Prayer at the foot of Half Dome in Yosemite, a great moment often occurs.

9. There She Was

"The secret of success is to do the common thing uncommonly well".
—John D. Rockefeller

During early sobriety, the men in recovery advised Charlie not to make any big decisions, such as getting into a relationship in the first year. Okay. Charlie was a patient man, and he could wait. After year one, Charlie said, "Okay, God, I'm ready. I need a girlfriend. I've got a year's sobriety, and I'm ready."

Year two passed, and Charlie asked, "God, where are you? No offense, but I am willing to be in a relationship now." His job at the airport only lasted about a year and a half because management fired him for refusing to take part in the party favors at the Christmas party on the company yacht in Marina Del Ray. The party with cocaine and hookers was going on below deck while Charlie stayed above deck and drank his ginger ale. He got fired for being a round peg in a square hole, and this time he was grateful for being fired.

Year three came around, and Charlie, literally on his knees, asked, "Okay God, this is getting ridiculous, where is she?"

They Already Were Acquainted

Charlie and Kerri shared the same friends and saw each other at social functions and at recovery meetings.

Their hometown was small and people ran into each other often. After a while, Charlie and Kerri started to notice each other. Kerri observed him through the time that he lost a job and was impressed with how he handled the situation. His character was positive. Charlie was true to his word, and people could depend on him. Kerri learned more about Charlie's resilience and can-do attitude, and she liked what she saw and felt.

Kerri often explained to her friends how natural Charlie was with her children, who were twins. "When Charlie was courting me, he appreciated the children. He enjoyed being with them and didn't treat them as a hassle. He also brought thoughtful gifts. Once, Charlie showed up with a video camera so that I could record the kids. I had nothing like that, and he was thoughtful in that way.

"He interacted with the kids, and they liked him a lot. On one of our first dates, his sponsor John Gale agreed to babysit while we went out. After we had left, the twins started throwing a tantrum. They jumped up and down and started screaming 'We want Mama. We want Mama!' John, being good with people, started jumping up and down screaming, 'I want Charlie, I want Charlie!' That surprised the twins so much that they calmed down. We came home to the twins fast asleep, and John reading from the Big Book.

"At that time, I had a job in which I occasionally traveled. Charlie stepped up and helped. During that time and while we were courting, he got a job transfer to the city of Arroyo Grande in California's Central Valley. We dated from a distance, which became more interesting with young children. I liked the Central Valley area. The twins were about three years old then, so I packed them in the car for our jaunts. Charlie found a daycare facility where the twins could play while I had to travel for work. We kept company with each other a lot, as we had so much fun. Charlie was always present for my children, and I appreciated that.

Kian and Kyla ready for Halloween in Montara
■

"When it was time to move forward in the relation-ship, Charlie, the twins, and I flew back to meet his mother and other family members on Signal Mountain and in Chatta-nooga. While we were there, Charlie took me up to a favorite childhood place to hang out on the mountain. It was a beauti-ful place right up from the house on the bluff of Signal Moun-tain overlooking the Tennessee River Valley. The place was special for Charlie, as he spent a lot of time with his friends there and felt a spiritual connection with the environmental beauty.

"Then, he asked me to marry him on Memorial Day in 2000, and I gladly accepted. Charlie had always envisioned a spectacular wedding, and that is what we had in Yosemite Valley, a place he loved. A charming chapel in the Valley is where he wanted to marry, and our backdrop would be the stunning landscape."

Only, There Was One Problem

"The night before the wedding, we had scheduled the rehearsal dinner. Charlie's family members arrived over the previous days. My friends from Southern California would be on their way. Or so I thought.

"We woke that next morning to an unimaginable surprise. The sky dumped over a foot and a half of snow and then dumped some more. The snow was deep by the time of the rehearsal dinner on the night before the wedding. Fortunately, most of the guests had arrived except one uncle from Southern California. The dinner was in the Mural Room at the Awanhee Lodge in Yosemite, and the tradition, history, and beauty were unsurpassed. The men stayed on to play poker and smoke cigars in the Starlight Room, with brother Kyle Kemp and best man Roger Berry playing high-stakes card games into the early morning. The women smartly went to their rooms to sleep.

"The day of the wedding was sunny and gorgeous. Yosemite Valley, after heavy snowfall on a sunny day, was spectacular with sparkles. My favorite wedding picture was of Charlie and me standing beneath a stately oak tree. The branches glistened with ice."

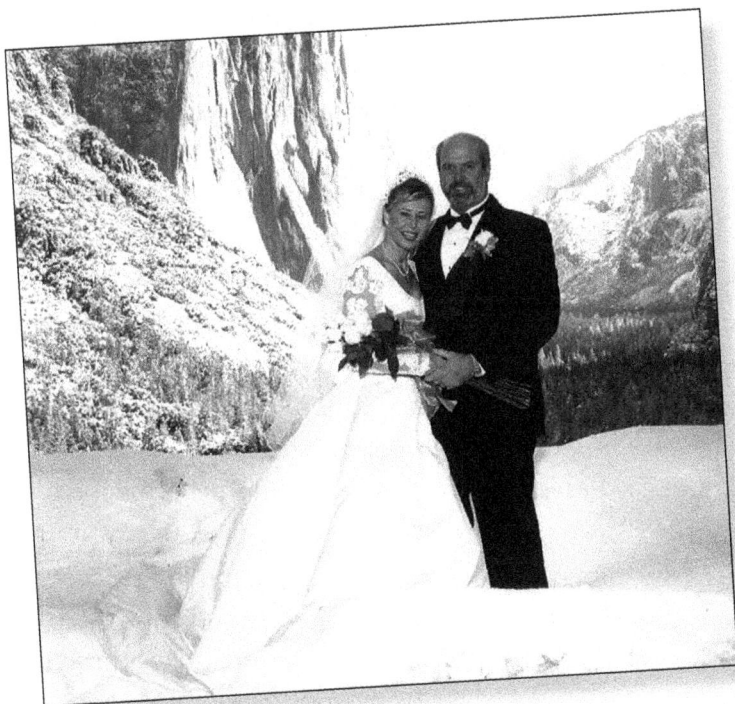

Wedding in Yosemite Valley ■

"Fortunately, I wore a long gown, which covered my snow boots underneath. Unfortunately for Charlie, he got cold feet. Not about the wedding, he literally got cold feet. He was wearing the rental dress shoes that complimented the tuxedo. The shoes were thin, and he nearly froze his toes off!

"When my turn came to enter the chapel, I walked out of the dressing room and stepped down. My foot slid on some ice, and I fell forward. Chris Gardner happened to be standing right where I was falling. He put his arms out and caught me. He was my hero that day. Otherwise, I would have walked into the chapel covered in mud and ice.

"The romantic wedding proceeded without a snag. My daughter was the flower girl, and my son was the ring-bearer. Charlie and I shared our vows, and then Charlie turned to the twins after we said our vows. He got down on one knee, took each child under an arm, and said in front of the audience, 'You guys just heard me promise to be your mom's husband, and be there for her. I promise you that I will be your Dad, and I will always be there for you.' And to spice things up a bit Charlie added, 'Now it's your turn to promise your Mother and I that you will always behave, and do everything we ask you to do. Say 'I do!" and they did, to everyone's amusement. It was even funnier that when we re-enacted the wedding on video one year later, the twins wised up and said, 'Dad, you tricked us!' To which Charlie replied, 'And now we have it on tape!'"

Charlie and Kerri had the honeymoon of their dreams. Charlie was three years sober, and Kerri was well along in recovery. They flew to French Polynesia and honeymooned in Bora Bora, an idyllic setting for a dream come true honeymoon with the romantic thatched hut and walks on the beach at sunset.

Adjusting to A Different Life

The family had planned to live in their home area in Half Moon Bay. Kerri had left her job to get married and moved down to Central California. The move to Arroyo Grande was temporary, and they expected to return to Half Moon Bay where the twins were enrolled in a special bilingual program and where Kerri planned to return to work.

Then, Charlie got a call out the blue. His employer wanted to transfer him to Baton Rouge, Louisiana, saying "Charlie, we've got one of those perfect opportunities for you. Rolling blackouts are hitting California because of the power grid restrictions by a power company out of Houston. Corporate headquarters in Omaha needs to get twenty people trained in how to build a power plant." The two projects included one outside of Kansas City and one outside of Baton Rouge, Louisiana. Charlie got the phone call, the opportunity, to take charge of the one in Baton Rouge.

Charlie was under pressure from the company to move. Kerri did not want to move and thought perhaps the distance could be managed. Their interrupted plans faded faster than either hoped. Charlie was adamant that they stay together rather than live apart for a while. Pressure mounted, and they found that in crisis, they couldn't talk through their process as a couple because the decision had to be fast. Kerri was not comfortable having decisions made for her after she relinquished her name, business, and the luxury of making decisions on her own. Having someone else make the decisions for her was foreign. However, at that time she didn't have a job and felt her only choice was to move.

The newlyweds packed up the kids, the dog, and the truck filled with the furniture and moved to Baton Rouge. The new Gardner family found a home there in June of 2001. Right off the bat, they noticed how different the culture was from California living. The people they met seemed overly religious and conservative. Those in their circle and neighborhood had not traveled out of the area much. Charlie and Kerri quickly discovered how cautious their neighbors were of Californians, and it was a challenge to adjust to the culture and language. Even Charlie, being from the South, understood that Cajun country was a world away from his Tennessee heritage and culture. Although Charlie could act as an interpreter, Kerri, being a Pasadena surfer girl, suffered from culture shock. To the Californians, who had funky accents, their neighbors had funky accents too.

Nine-Eleven Changed Everything

The phone rang, and Kerri said, "Hi Charlie. What's up?"

His voice cracked when he said, "Kerri, turn on the television." She turned it on in time to see the second plane hit the second tower in New York. They were both upset and worried. They lived in an area between Baton Rouge and all the way down to New Orleans. This corridor was home to chemical and petrol refineries. Those, who lived there nicknamed that corridor Cancer Alley, as all the chemical plants had relocated there from California and other places due to "relaxed regulations." People in the community feared further terrorist sabotage and possible chemical leaks, which, as it turned out, did not occur.

The twins Kian and Kyla had a fifth birthday coming up, and Charlie arranged to fly the family to Disney World in Florida the week after 9/11. They had a strange, yet memorable and fun adventure. What was strange was the entire park was empty, completely devoid of customers. What was incredible for them was no long lines to get on rides. They could ride as many times as they liked. Charlie, Kerri, and the twins went through most all of the three parks in three days and saw all the exhibits. However, the park having no visitors was a memory they wanted to forget, but couldn't.

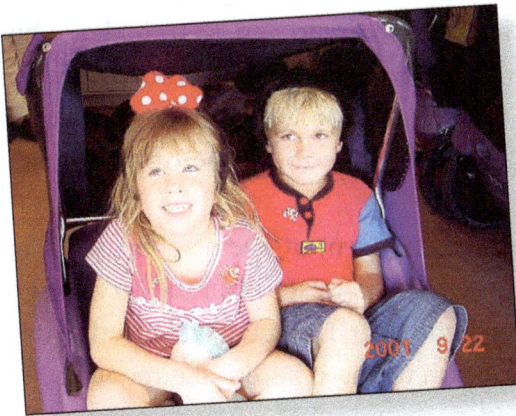

The twins Kian and Kyla at Disneyworld 2001.
∎

Good Neighbor Policy

In one conversation with neighbors, who were local indigenous Cajuns, Kerri commented, "In Baton Rouge, I've noticed that there a lot of black people. Where we live out here in Livingston Parish, there seem to be no black people. What's going on with that?"

"Well," an older neighbor spoke up. "Don't you know, child? You're in David Duke country."

"Who's David Duke?" Kerri asked.

Charlie chimed in, "Uh-oh. David Duke is the Grand Imperial Wizard of the Ku Klux Klan."

The neighbor agreed, "Ain't no black people goin' be livin' 'round here."

After that conversation, Charlie wondered if it was wise for the family to stay. The twins were just starting kindergarten, and he had to consider Kerri. Charlie could tolerate the culture because of his Southern upbringing. Not Kerri. The cultural shift was affecting their marriage. Kerri had quit her job to follow his career, but the cultural shock rocked both of them. They couldn't find suitable recovery meetings, and they agreed if something didn't change soon, one of them might likely drink again.

A miracle came in the form of one neighbor noticing the newlywed's dilemma and suggested that they try the Friday Eatin' Meetin across the river. This meeting invited all joiners to bring a pot-luck dish to share before the meeting. The food was all fried, but it was good! The couple enjoyed the camaraderie and hung out with the group until the day the twins got out of the first semester of kindergarten around Christmas.

By then, the family was packed and ready to leave. They left the boat behind and spent the next night across the border in Texas. Finally, they were on the way back to California. They felt free and ready for some fun. Unfortunately, the feeling was short-lived. Charlie thought a fun adventure while in route would be to cross the border in El Paso and travel into the sister city of Juarez, Mexico to spend the night. This decision wasn't so smart. Their car, like hundreds of others, crossed the bridge and came to the entry point. The car was in the parking queue, unable to turn back, when they finally saw the big sign: DO NOT BRING GUNS INTO MEXICO!

Charlie realized he had his Browning Hi-Power with him. He had been brought up by his dad with a genuine respect for firearms and gun safety. He had previously been issued a concealed carry permit when he and Roger lived in Virginia, and carried with him this time while traveling across country. He grew up with the training that one did not go out into the woods without protection, and going across country with his new family warranted that same protection. Being from Tennessee, he was naturally a good shot.

There was nothing they could do about it, and they entered Juarez. Charlie realized they were not in the safest of neighborhoods, so he got a hotel room and hunkered down with his wife and the twins. The next morning, as they attempted to cross back into the US, their German Shepherd, Tasha, went into protective mode and barked at the Border Patrol officers. They ordered Charlie to pull over for a search while Kerri and the kids watched in fear. Thoughts of rotting in a Mexican jail cell flooded Charlie's mind, but when he managed to get Tasha under control, the Border Patrol finally let them through and they drove straight home.

Santa Murphy

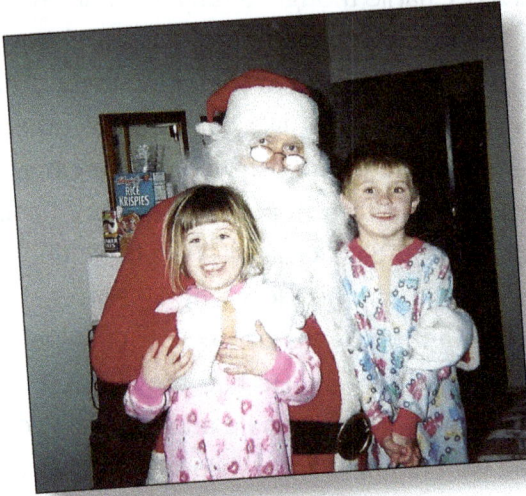

Santa Murphy makes a visit
■

The family ended up being in Baton Rouge for about nine months before returning to Half Moon Bay. They lived out of a hotel for about two weeks while school was out because their properties still had tenants who had not moved out yet. This meant they spent Christmas of 2002 in a hotel room. Christmas Eve came when, suddenly, they heard jingle bells and a hearty "Ho Ho Ho" coming up the hallway. Santa Claus came knocking on their door, and the children's wide eyes sparkled in amazement. Santa brought the exact toys they wanted for Christmas. The twins couldn't figure out how Santa found them, let alone brought them exactly what they wanted. Charlie replied, "Don't you know? Santa sees every-thing." The twins were still a little suspicious when their friend Murphy went riding off on a motorcycle with no reindeer. ■

10. Establishing a Family Life

The family moved into Charlie's home in Montara when his job required that he drive some distance for the project. He commuted several hours each day to one job in Manteca. Finally, his employer put an RV on the job site for Charlie to stay during the week and come home on the weekends. The company, Peter Kiewit Sons, also scheduled quarterly district-wide safety meetings for employees. The safety meeting was for all supervisory personnel to review work safety initiatives, and review project safety records. Everybody in the company from foreman up to the Division Manager of the Northern California District was expected to attend, and those with no recordable injuries on their job sites were recognized.

Instilling that core value in all work sites was the belief that you can work a complete job without any injuries. As a project manager, Charlie had an initial conversation with each employee that he managed. This conversation stated that they each had the authority to stop the work if one saw a condition that was not right, or to point out and question if someone did not understand. Not only did each employee have the authority to stop the work, but each also had the responsibility to stop the work, make it right and make it safe.

.

The Truest of Miracles

One morning, Charlie chose to drive his Ford F-150 truck, instead of the company vehicle, because it was more comfortable. He could cruise along, listen to his favorite CDs, such as Dave Koz or Mindi Abair, and arrive an hour later relaxed and alert. The company sponsored a breakfast meeting at 8:00 am.

Charlie's route involved driving along the Devils' Slide, treacherous, cliff-hanging road along the Pacific Coast Highway. That morning, the bluff had thick fog and the road was wet in this area. Charlie spotted an older man driving toward him. The man had failed to slow down and did not see the upcoming hairpin curves. He crossed over into Charlie's lane, crashed into the k-rail, and slid down the rail toward Charlie's car.

Then Charlie did the first thing that he had always been told never to do: Don't swerve to miss the deer because that's when people run off the road and bad accidents happen.

Well, Charlie surmised he had the ability and space to swerve inside, on the side closest to the bluff and possibly, he might miss the oncoming driver. However, the other driver had a Dodge Ram 2500 compared to Charlie's smaller Ford F-150. Charlie dodged to the inside, the oncoming Dodge Ram popped off the k-rail, and collided head-on with a crash loud enough to slam his ears. The older man lifted Charlie's truck up and drove it backward about 10 feet along the k-rail. Charlie looked down at the water 800 feet straight below him, and he knew he was going over. His heart fluttered, and mind panicked– O God, I'm going over. I am going to die. This truck is going to tumble down this cliff.

People get severely hurt or killed if they are thrown from a vehicle or try to jump out of it when it is falling over a cliff. Charlie made a split-second decision to get out of the truck and grab hold of something to prevent sliding down the bluff. He did try opening the door, but to no avail. Then he noticed that white gray smoke poured from the dashboard. He struggled to get out because the truck was going to blow. Instantaneously, time slowed down. Actions became exaggerated as seconds turned to minutes. Charlie knew this warp in time was shock and an up-leveling of the brain to cope and survive. The experience of looking down at the ocean and realizing that he was about to die made Charlie think: Why am I dying? It is okay because I know where I am going? But why now?

What an odd surprise that Charlie remembered an incident from childhood, watching a memory like a movie. He was about fourteen years-old when the family cat got caught in the new trash compacter. Charlie and his mom heard that cat howling, and his mom turned the compacter off. They didn't know at that time if the compactor cycle was still on the way down or was coming back up. They opened the door as wide as possible, but the opening was a sliver, maybe an inch and a half wide. They thought the cat wouldn't make it out. However, fear is a marvelous motivator. That cat squeezed through, popped out of the trash compacter, and ran away.

Charlie's brain motivated him to similar action. He

pushed on the car door again. The door opened only the sliver, and this large man, six-foot-plus and 250 pounds, squeezed out of what he thought was the burning car. In the slowed motion, seeing black and white only, Charlie strode around to the back of the truck and noticed the other driver was stumbling in a daze from his truck. Behind the driver, oncoming cars were still rolling around the bluff only to screech to abrupt halts and crash into the rear of the other driver's car. That driver needed to get off the road and away from his car. Still moving in slow motion and seeing black and white, Charlie went to the other driver and physically moved him out of the oncoming traffic to the side of the road. The paramedics finally arrived and Charlie explained his vision was seeing black and white, no color. The paramedics said, "Not to worry, you are just in shock. The first thing to go is color. Your optic nerve gets overloaded with sensory input. The next phase of shock is that everything slows down because an overloaded brain is trying to process."

Other drivers pulled up and one person got out to help. Charlie asked him, "Look, there's no phone reception here. Can you drive down the street and call my wife Kerri to let her know what's happened?" The helpful driver did call Kerri, and she and the twins walked up to the accident scene. Kerri gazed at the Devil's Slide where Charlie almost went over and fell in a swoon. The paramedics, who worked on Charlie, left him and went to assist Kerri.

In the meantime, Charlie was nursing a sprained wrist because he had been holding a cup of coffee in the air as he drove. When the accident happened, the airbag deployed and blew the cup of coffee into the back seat along with pulling his arm backward. Charlie was amazed he survived.

Moreover, he so was full of gratitude for being alive, that he started to question why? Sure, random accidents happened. Yet, the fact that he, a man of height and size, could squeeze out of the car, kept him wondering about why he lived instead of tumbling down the rocks. The whole event was miraculous to Charlie.

However, just two days later, he started having trouble walking, and the hip joints were painful. His primary care physician was cautious about the injury and suggested, "Sometimes it takes a while for these things to release after a trauma like your accident. Let's keep an eye on it." In the meantime, the doctor promised that he would continue to monitor Charlie's mobility.

Bridging the Gap

Right about the same time as I had hip replacement surgery, I lost two of the most influential people in my life. John Gale, my first Sponsor and mentor, and my Mom.

John was one of the most quirky, irascible people I ever met. He was a used car salesman that had been fired from practically every used car dealership in the Bay Area. He was known around the recovery rooms as a perineal "13th stepper" which meant he hit on every woman that came into the rooms, a fact that was well known and he was pretty much harmless. But when it came to the program of recovery, he was dead serious. He knew the Book and the literature as well as anybody, and applied it to his life. He saved my life. They say when the student is ready, the teacher will arrive, and I met John when I needed help the most. John got cancer, and it came on quick, hard, and merciless. By the time it was detected, it had metastasized and spread beyond repair, and he was given 3 months to live.

I've always been fascinated by the grace and dignity some people with a terminal illness can conduct themselves amidst such dire circumstances, not all do, but John applied the principles of acceptance and was amazing up to the end. I've wondered if I would have the courage to do what John did. Anyway, I recall a time when I was scheduled to have a "special day" with my son, Kian, and called to cancel as I needed to see John while I still could. I called Kian and told him what I was going to do, and he said he wanted to go too. I told him John's condition, that he was near death and it was not pretty, but he insisted on going.

When we got to where John was staying, on the beach in Santa Cruz where he grew up, it was obvious the time was near. After some small talk, not knowing what to say, I asked him, "John, Kian insisted coming today. Here he is at 13 years of age. What would you tell a young man as you are getting near making the next transition?" I wish I had recorded the next 5 minutes because it was the most beautiful, eloquent speech I believe I ever had heard.

John talked about what a wonderful blessing this thing called Life is, that we are lucky to have the opportunity to walk through this delicate journey and we should experience this thing with gratitude. I watched my son enthralled with the talk, and our special day turned into a special moment. I remember this moment as a milestone when my son was becoming a man. I'll always remember John in the recovery meetings, and he will live on as long as I do on this earth.

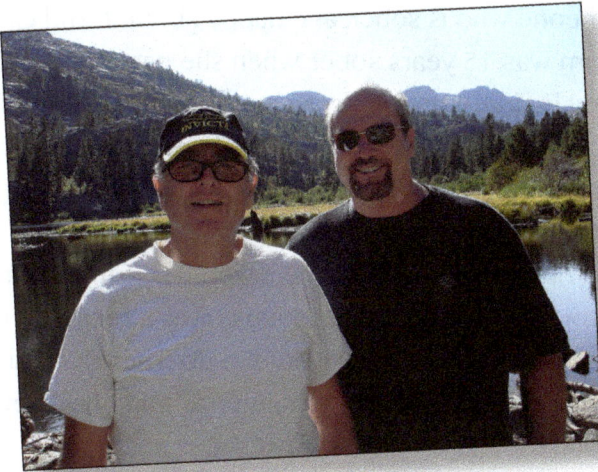

John Gale and I in Tahoe ■

Then one day, I received a call from brother Ellis that Mom was about to go. I remember her telling me that "The World is a different place when your mother is not in it." She had been told that by her mother, and I think she was preparing me for the ultimate severing of the umbilical cord.

Mom had worked hard and wanted to leave her boys a small inheritance. To reassure her that her sons would be all right, I told her, "Mom, I am going to take what money you leave and use it to buy a house in Lake Tahoe. We're going to have a family reunion there, at least every other year. That way we'll come together. We'll stay together, and we'll honor you. Because the house will be dedicated to you."

I Followed Through On That Promise

I've heard it said around recovery meetings that a winner is someone who is sober, and happy about it, and can die sober. Mom was 15 years sober when she passed.

Several hundred people from her community attended her funeral because she was so well-respected and well liked. Her pastor said, "You know, Mary Leavell was a very special lady for all of us in the community." The pastor came to her just before she passed, and he asked her if there was anything he could do for her. Her response was strength personified: "No, there's nothing that you can do. There's no sin that I have not confessed. There's no amends that I have left to make.

I'm ready to go."

... and with that, two of the most important people in my life went to that other place we go. A place where I believe is no more pain, no more anguish, and all is well.

Compatibility Issues

Kerri and Charlie settled into their living routines with their children. Kerri stayed home to care for the children and ran the household. Charlie worked on his job site during the week and came home on the weekend. Family routines were disrupted, and arguments followed. Conflict resonated with them more than love or communication. They weren't working as a couple at that point. While they had their personal conflicts and angry scenarios, the last straw for Kerri was watching young Kian curl into a fetal position on the floor during an argument. Divorce was eminent.

The couple talked with a divorce mediator to work through issues. Charlie and Kerri eventually separated, and since they lived in a small community, it was not easy. At first, their separation was awkward because they shared close friends, and they determined together not to carry the pain and anger forward. They would not go there with each other or their children. Charlie and the kids wanted involvement, as did Kerri.

Eventually, once they got through that hard part with the divorce, they started to be friends. They participated in their communities and could be in the same place at the same time and be comfortable. Charlie was glad for that. Both of them were working forward, trying to be positive, and not have a negative outcome. He wanted to take the kids to the movies, and enjoy hockey games, dinners in a nice restaurant and the occasional travel and shopping. Kerri and Charlie have both been there for the twins, and Charlie declared that he still was and will always be.

When Charlie started dating again and met Marina some time before he got sick, Kerri and the twins met her and liked her. When the twins visited him, Marina was also there sometimes, and they enjoyed spending time with each other. Kerri, the twins, and Charlie made smooth transitions when the anger and hurt were healing. ■

11. Reconstruction of Hip and Life

Fall seven times and stand up eight
—Japanese Proverb

Six months later, Charlie's hip joints were worse, which warranted an MRI at Seton Hospital in Bailey City. After the magnetic resonance imaging scans, the doctor sat down to discuss the condition with Charlie.

"You're going to need a new hip," The doctor bluntly told him. "The accident fractured the cartilage in your hip, like just fractured it. Your femur is growing into your hip bone, which is making it become arthritic. That explains the pain you're in."

Charlie sat for a moment, thinking through the ramifications of this surgery.

"So, tell me, Charlie, what kind of hip do you want?" The doctor interrupted Charlie's thoughts. "We can give you a fiberglass hip that can get you through all the security at the airport. On the other hand, are you active?"

"Yeah, I still go skiing with Marina."

"If you're skiing with a fiberglass hip, and you have an accident, you could shatter your hip and be back in here."

"No, I don't want to do that."

"Well, then we can give you the Cadillac version. It's the two-inch ball titanium hip. It will not shatter. In fact, you'll probably die with it in place."

Charlie went ahead with the surgery, anxious to have it over with and to literally be back on his feet again. Charlie stayed awake through surgery. The doctor had to cut through a lot of muscle and nerve to get to the bone, but they numbed the lower body so he wouldn't feel anything. He was told that he could expect to lose feeling in the area. The surgeon removed the bone from the hip socket with the same device auto mechanics use to extract gears from a car's transmission. The doctor amputated the bone about eight inches down; then put a metal spike down into the leg bone. Next the surgeon fixed a big, gnarly socket of titanium that fits back into the hip socket. Voila! Charlie had a new, titanium hip, and did not realize that it would take at least six months for feeling to return to the area. Yet, Charlie was up and walking with a cane and walker within a matter of a week. The hospital made Charlie their poster child because the operation was successful, and he was back to work sooner than most. They took pictures of him showcasing his successful recovery in his hardhat and displayed them throughout the orthopedic ward.

When Charlie went into the operation, he prayed incessantly. Specifically, he asked that His will be done, as he could surrender and accept the situation without fear. When the doctor came in and was getting ready for the operation, he asked the nurse, "Have you sedated Charlie yet.?"

"No, we are about to do so."

"Charlie seems very calm for not having had the sedation."

Charlie chimed in at that point, "It is because I am praying."

"Well, it is working," the doctor said. "When you get a

hip replacement, a nurse or therapist will get you up that day."
Charlie woke up after the hip surgery, and the nurse said,

"Are you ready to stand up?"

"Stand up? I don't know..."

The nurse, without hesitation, took Charlie's hand and guided him to stand. His sweaty efforts felt as if he had worked out for two hours.

"All right", said the nurse, "That's enough for now. You'll be able to do more later."

Cocky Charlie, who was sweating bullets and huffing, said, "Oh, that was easy. What do I have to do to get out of here?"

The nurse replied in a reasonable tone, "Well, you have to walk and complete one circle around the hospital floor. Then, you should go up and down the stairs. Finally, you have to have a bowel movement."

"Heck. That's simple. I'll be out of here tomorrow." Charlie always was an optimist. Four days later, however, he was sitting on the toilet groaning, "Ah, come on." The opioids they had given for pain constipated his system.

Walking around the hospital floor was a long journey over four days. On day one, Charlie walked twenty steps. Did God foresee that Charlie would need this same persistent character traits to learn to walk again after the sepsis episode?

Earthquake!

During his hip recovery, Kerri had brought the twins

by on a regular basis to see their dad. One day when Charlie and Kian were visiting, a substantial earthquake rocked the Seton-Daily City Hospital.

Someone ran down the hall, going from door-to-door, yelling, "Get out of the hospital. Earthquake! Get out. Hurry." Charlie began yelling back, "I can't move! I just had a hip replaced! "

The halls of the hospital emptied quickly. Understandably, no one came to help Charlie or Kian. Seton Daily City was built in the 1970s with the latest features in earthquake resistance. The foundation was on rollers! As it turns out, the rollers were worse in earthquakes. The earthquake they felt was a strong 6.0. Moreover, the hospital was within a quarter mile of the San Andreas Fault. The building shook like crazy, but neither Charlie nor Kian were hurt. Kian was already leery of elevators. After the quake, he was no longer interested in coming to visit his dad at that hospital.

Charlie's Mom's Passed

Like her dad and the generations before them, Charlie's mom was an alcoholic. She eventually got sober and maintained her sobriety. She knew that Charlie had an alcohol problem and tried to help him get sober in the late 1990s. She had been telling Roger Berry, who was already sober, that Charlie was the person they should help. "Charlie's got a drinking problem. We have to help him," she told Roger.

Mom sometimes called Charlie and recited the Serenity Prayer over the phone. After several calls, Charlie asked her to leave him alone, as it happened too often and it made him uncomfortable. However, when Charlie became ready for sobriety, the first step was to surrender. He went to Roger's home in Phoenix for the first 30-days of surrender because he had been evicted from his house and had no place to go. For the second thirty days, he went home to his mom in Tennessee. Then, he went back to the San Francisco Bay area and stayed with Tom and Lisa Hanley in Berkeley because he wanted to live in that area.

Mom Was a Survivor

Mom was a breast cancer survivor for forty years after having a radical mastectomy in the 1960s. Then the cancer returned. As she described her condition to Charlie, she told him she "got the bad cancer, and did radical therapy and radiation until I was drained and worn out."

At the time of her worsening condition, Charlie was running a large project up in Petaluma, north of the Bay area. The Gardner family members decided to have a small family reunion to go to Tennessee and say their goodbyes to mom. She was hanging on, but also worried about how her boys were going to survive after her death. Would they get along? Would there be bickering? Charlie just reminded her, "Mom you don't have anything to worry about. We're going to do just fine."

Mom had worked hard and wanted to leave her boys

a small inheritance. To reassure her that her sons would be all right, Charlie told her, "Mom, I am going to take what money you leave and use it to buy a house in Lake Tahoe. We're going to have a family reunion there, at least every other year. That way we'll come together. We'll stay together, and we'll honor you. Because the house will be dedicated to you." Charlie followed through on that promise.

The pastor came to her just before she passed, and he asked her if there was anything he could do for her. Her response was strength personified: "No, there's nothing that you can do. There's no sin that I have not confessed. There's no amends that I have left to make. I'm ready to go." That was a beautiful moment.

She surrendered, and had nothing left to do on this earth.

Several hundred people from her community attended her funeral because she was so well-respected and well liked. Her pastor said, "You know, Mary Leavell was a very special lady for all of you in the community."

All four Gardner brothers cherished their mother. What resilience she had to raise four boys. Her tenacity kept food on the family table and brought the family closer in knowing they were cared for. No family member could have guessed that just three years later, they would face the possibility that another family member might die. ∎

12. The Possibility of Charlie's Death

**"Faith is not knowing what the future holds,
but knowing Who holds the future"**
—Solomon

Over the seemingly endless six weeks, Steve Wilson, Charlie's long-time friend in recovery, was one of the first people who visited Charlie in the Intensive Care Unit at Mills-Peninsula Hospital. Charlie had not yet recovered from the sepsis that had triggered his organ failure and a comatose state.

Steve later told Charlie that he kept a daily vigil by coming straight from work to the hospital. A communication network was set up by the three brothers, Roger, Kerri, Marina, and Steve. They were in communication by email or phone regularly. If there were any changes in Charlie's condition, they asked: What do we need? Are things taken care of? They were all checking in with each other to ensure everyone had what they needed.

Day-by-day they kept their vigilance and communication.

Someone was with Charlie all the time. His brothers, Chris and Ellis, frequently slept next to Charlie's bed on the window seat, or else they would stretch out their chair and put their feet up on the corner of the bed and go to sleep. Tommy arrived when that final crucial decision had to be made and Marina and Kerri and the twins visited every day.

Soon Charlie had more frequent visits from his friends in recovery. People from his church also stopped by to pray over him. Steve was sure that had an effect, and thought that everyone's prayer had a lot to do with his recovery.

Some decisions were made on a collaborative basis. Usually, the Gardner brothers made the important decisions, and sometimes, they might consult Steve as well. He had a secondary role in Charlie's estate plan, which his law partner had drawn up for Charlie. Unknown to Steve, however, for a while at least, Charlie had made Steve his secondary trustee in case Ellis could not serve in that role.

When the initial surprise of the news about Charlie subsided, the events surrounding Charlie and friends and family members fell into a rhythm. The financial issues were covered. Conversations with hospital staff were frequent, and still, their friend and brother didn't seem to improve. They reached a very tense time in his hospitalization, and all of them were deeply disturbed that they were coming to this point. The decision would have to be forthcoming as to whether or not to continue Charlie's life support or to remove the tubes because the doctor's told us Charlie's brain had flat-lined, and that they should not expect improvement.

Charlie had a Do-Not-Resuscitate instruction in his will, which was a current document. His brothers had the primary role in this. They were going to approach this on a collaborative basis because no one was going to let any one person take sole responsibility for this life-ending decision.

"All of us tried absolutely everything we knew to get Charlie to wake up". His visitors talked to him, sang to him, prayed in his ear, offered conversations, and read books to him. Each done did whatever they could to get eyelid movement, or muscle movement, or any indication of consciousness in any way. The reality was that horrible muscle atrophy set in as the result of Charlie's body lying in a hospital bed for six weeks without moving. The body makes a last-ditch effort to find and kill the infection and ends up eating away at its muscles. E-mails that passed among Charlie's brothers told the tale:

"They're setting up for the EEG now and will take a spinal tap later today most likely. The EEG may or may not shed some light on neurological function. The spinal tap is to check for infections in the central nervous system."

"However, overall, the last 24 hours have been disappointing. Charlie is fighting to get oxygenation even though the lung X-rays show improvement. Continued infection was ongoing. Having already been on antibiotics, it makes culture results unclear. The likelihood of "false negative" is quite high for the condition. Therefore, doctors administered massive doses of generalized antibiotics. Other signs of Charlie's distress were a high heart rate and low blood pressure."

"The doctor said that Charlie had gone from dangerous to worse. The most frightening indicator was over-the-top potassium levels. They increased dramatically. Potassium comes from cell death and increases when fighting off infections (cells are dying in that process) so we expect some growth. However, his levels are 2-3 times higher than anticipated and showed that other tissue cells and organ cells are dying. This was a bad sign. Hope was dim and fading for Charlie to recover to anything that resembled his former self."

Charlie's brothers followed each step and were glad they monitored medication levels and procedures because of the mistakes that were made. For example, the doctors attached three ports to Charlie's arms in order to be able to administer medications into the bloodstream directly. Another one went through Charlie's chest directly into his heart. Overall, the shunts remained in Charlie for two months. A nurse or doctor would have to check them, and they cleaned and replaced the shunts on several occasions.

One doctor checked the port in the chest, and his face turned ashen. An emergency occurred when the pic line installed into the heart slipped out of the heart and became wedged into Charlie's heart valve. The condition could have caused a stroke or a heart attack at any moment. The replacement of the pic line was an emergency situation. Family members had to wonder why someone made that mistake, and moreover, got away with the error with no reprimand. The doctor, nurses, and friends discussed how Charlie must be on his deathbed. After all, a doctor had induced his coma over a month ago. They acknowledged that they had tried everything. They had pumped all the antibiotics they had into his system.

The Truth Was Dismal

Charlie's brain and body were not responsive to treatment. His kidneys had failed. His liver had failed. His lungs could collapse at any time.

The doctors had Charlie on the drug Propofol, which slowed the activity of the brain and nervous systems. A surgeon might use this medication before and during surgery to help a patient relax. The drug seemed to wipe the memory centers by decreasing levels of consciousness. The doctor took two to three X-rays a day of Charlie's chest to watch the lung's progression to failure. Near the end, the lungs showed as a white mass of infection.

Ellis had the power of attorney for Charlie. He was laden with the responsibility to talk with the three doctors and notify them of the family's preferences. He worked closely and communicated with the emergency care physician, Dr. Steyer. And since Ellis didn't want Charlie to hear, he went out into the hallway to talk with the doctor. Chris and Roger joined them.

"You know doctor," Ellis started, "that I am responsible for saying when we are at the point of no return, or Charlie's a vegetable. How do we know when to pull the plug? How does it all work?"

The doctor had answered this question before, and Ellis never realized how barbaric and straightforward the procedure would be. They would take Charlie off the machines, as they had intubated Charlie and were giving him oxygen since he arrived.

The doctor explained, "Charlie's oxygen level has come back, and his lungs are working on their own. The point of taking the tube out of his throat is to see if Charlie survives,"

"I thought that would be the point that Charlie died.

Doctor, Charlie smoked for about thirty years. I want to know if he has lung cancer?"

"No, no lung cancer at all," the doctor reassured him.

Pull the Plug or Not

The pneumonia was cleared up by all the antibiotics within a week of Charlie's arrival at ICU. It was the sepsis that appeared terminal. Ellis wanted to keep Charlie on the machines at least until Tommy arrived. Ellis communicated with Tommy all along because Tommy had more experience in hospitals with his son. He knew the questions to ask the doctors to get accurate answers.

Ellis made calls to those who had supported Charlie so well, and told them that tomorrow the doctors wanted to pull the plug. They said Charlie's brain was disorganized. One doctor took his car key and jabbed it hard into Charlie's foot. The doctor wanted a reaction, and there was absolutely nothing. The doctor was checking for a reflex again, and still, nothing was happening. ∎

13. Charlie Rises in Light

"Carve your name on hearts, not tombstones. A legacy is etched into the minds of others and the stories they share about you." —Shannon L. Alder

---

Those friends and family members in the room feared that this was the end. They had watched Charlie for weeks as he lay in a non-responsive coma. That night the doctors convinced Charlie's brothers that it was time to pull the plug. At around midnight, Ellis phoned Kerri and told her to bring the twins to say goodbye to their dad.

We Got the Call

Kerri brought the twins, Kyla and Kian, to see their dad. They were at the tender age of fifteen. By this time, the children and Kerri had not missed one day of the last six weeks that Charlie was hospitalized. The twins were frightened that Charlie might die.

Ellis called them around ten o'clock that night, July 25, 2011, and said they were going to pull the plug the next day. That we should come now and say goodbye. The time was near.

Kerri and the children went up to the ICU to talk to Charlie. Kerri had been telling Kyla all along, "Honey, we don't know what's going to happen here. You need to talk to Charlie now. We don't know if he comes-to whether or not he's going to remember anybody. You need to just talk to him, in case, you know, he dies."

Kyla was adamant that she would not speak with him until he could talk back. For these past weeks, every time they visited Charlie, Kyla would not talk to him. She might say hello and then go into her corner. She'd sit there in silence, and this worried Kerri as a mother. Kyla and Charlie had always been close. Kian and Kerri were worried about her possible well-being if Charlie passed away.

Kerri spoke to Charlie, and Kian spoke with him also. They each had good memories to recall, and Kerri asked Kyla how she would feel if Charlie didn't regain consciousness and she had never talked to him again? Well, knowing that they were going to pull the plug, and Charlie likely would die, Kyla decided she had a lot to say to Charlie that night.

Kian and Kerri curled up on the couch and dozed a bit, while Kyla spent a lot of time talking to Charlie. Crying... she told him she wanted him to come back...that she was going to miss him.

"Dad, you promised to walk me down the aisle when I get married. Who's going to do that? You said you'd give me my high school diploma. Who will take your place on the school board?" Kyla was sobbing. Her heart was breaking. At least she got to say goodbye.

What happened next was a total surprise. A nurse came in and jabbed Charlie hard in the stomach with one of the medicines, and he flinched! Charlie flinched. He felt it!

Kerri quickly dialed the brothers, who were having

dinner, and said, "Something's different. He flinched! I've never seen him flinch. He flinched."

They were all excited about that, but they also knew that they were still going to pull the plug.

Kerri went over to Charlie and walloped him in the shoulder and said, "Okay, you son of a bitch. If you're going to come back, you need to return now. They're pulling the plug tomorrow!" She slapped him on his face as if he would come out of the coma. She figured she had nothing to lose. Maybe if Charlie heard his ex-wife nagging him and hitting him, he might respond. However, it didn't happen that night. The twins and Kerri cried the whole way home and then cried themselves to sleep.

Death Happens

In the ICU where Charlie was, a cacophony of beeps from his surrounding meters sounded the warning of distress. Acute Respiratory Tension Syndrome took effect while Charlie convulsed. Marina noticed his sedation medication had come unhooked and was dripping on the floor. Nurses tried to reconnect the tube that delivered Propofol, which had disconnected from the stint in Charlie's arm. His blood pressure shot above 255 while followed by thirteen consecutive Myocardial Infarctions (strokes). The doctor and several nurses hurried franticly to stabilize Charlie's brain and body.

The doctor told the brothers, "It is time to pull the plug. He's a vegetable, and his Do-Not-Resuscitate order

states he doesn't want to live like that, so pull the plug."
Pull the plug? Just like flipping a switch. Turning out a light.

Dark
Done
Dead

Looking back, Charlie recalls that his brother Ellis was the appointed Power of Attorney and was worn down by the constant barrage of bad news, faint hope, and the always something worse. By that time, four weeks into Charlie's comatose state, all of his organs had failed. The lungs functioned at three percent with the ventilator. Then came the diagnosis of no brain activity. Charlie was dead.

One neurologist, Dr. Steyer, thought that if they took Charlie off the sedation, pulled the tube out of the trachea, and he could breathe on my own, perhaps there would be brain activity. What the family agreed to do was to call Kerri and the twins to say their goodbyes, as this would be the last time they get to speak with dad. At midnight, Kian went in first and talked for about twenty minutes. He'd been coming to visit every night for the last six weeks and had processed what is going on.

Kyla was reluctant as she had maintained a stance that she would not talk to Charlie until he could talk with her! Every night for the past four weeks, she couldn't bear to look at Charlie's swollen body, so she just waved a quick hello and found consolation in her PlayStation world. But that night would have been her last time to say goodbye because the plug would be pulled in the morning. Slowly Kyla told Charlie about how she would miss the times Charlie promised he would be there, like giving her the diploma for graduating high school; walking her down the aisle when she gets married; and paying for a big outrageous honeymoon. Kyla cried at the pain of loss that comes from loving opportunities.

Out of My Body, I Saw the Light

At this point, Charlie was floating out of his body and up to a bluish white light, which was extremely bright, but didn't hurt his eyes to see it. He felt peaceful because several shadowy beings at his side shepherded him toward the light saying, "Do not fear. You are where you are supposed to be."

Suddenly, Charlie realized he was dying. He was still in the ICU hovering over his body, but felt he had to move out of the way and could see better from the corner of the room. As the twins came to say goodbye, he started to be lifted. He rested in what felt like a giant catcher's mitt and was slowly moved up toward a light that emanated peace and warmth. Then he relaxed. Charlie was dying and consciously watching the process.

So, this is what dying is like?

Why am I dying?

Well, I guess it's okay, because I know where I'm going.

Charlie had a strong sense of faith; he believes in the Lord Jesus Christ, in God, and in Heaven. He knew he will be in Heaven as promised by Christ. As soon as he had that thought, suddenly, the surroundings changed. He was floating in bluish water of what seemed to be plasma bubbles. He had a passing thought about being in the womb and felt so peaceful. What he guessed must be the Pearly Gates looked to be blue pearl-shaped balls that appeared as little dimensions all to themselves. They surrounded him, like he was in a sea of Nerf balls. He recognized the crucial moment of God's tremendous presence. It was everywhere. Then he was inundated with impressions and sounds. A chorus of angels sang a familiar tune. More importantly, he heard Kyla crying. He had turned to hear the crying and was whooshed immediately down a wormhole.

Poof!

Charlie eyes opened in what to him were the next few seconds, but I later learned that the process in earth time was actually a week and a half later.

Tommy Gardner

Due to obligations at work, Tommy finally arrived later than his brothers. When he walked into the hospital room, he swore that Charlie's eyes followed him across the room when he set his stuff down. He approached the bed and saw that Charlie's eyes were open and he could see the pupils follow him around. Tommy had to ask, "Why are we pulling the plug? Is Charlie brain dead?"

The neurologist came into the room to answer the

question. "Yes, we ran this test, which is foolproof. You hold Charlie's hand above his head as he's lying there. If his brain has functions, Charlie's reflex will warn him not to let the hand hit his head and will jerk the arm away."

"Really? That's funny."

"Yeah, let me show you." The doctor held Charlie's hand above his head. He drops it, and it misses.

He said, "Well, I'm not holding it right." So, he held the hand above the head again, he dropped it, and it missed again. Tommy said, "Well, doc, do you want me to hold it over his head?"

"No, my mistake." The doctor did this five times, and Charlie's hand hadn't hit his head yet.

"So, doc, from what you're telling me, Charlie's got brain function."

"No, we did all these checks"

"Well, it's not checking out now."

The embarrassed doctor scratched his head and ran off. Tommy looked at Charlie's charts again. He and Ellis talked about it until a different doctor walked in and addressed them. The doctor explained it this way, "No, his eyes are following you purely from reflexes. There's no brain function. His eyes just follow a moving object because that's what they're trained to do. You know, that's his brain stem, but it's not brain function. Pay no attention to that."

Tommy said to Ellis, "Let's give it another day. You know, Charlie seems to be getting better. The insurance is covering it. What's one more day?"

"That's fine with me."

Several doctors came back to tell us, "No. You guys got it wrong. He doesn't need another day. We've already decided."

"Well, I think I'm the one who has power of attorney," Ellis responded. "I think I get to decide." Ellis' statement encouraged the doctors to give Charlie one more day. Legally, Ellis was right.

When Tommy saw Charlie the next day, Charlie's eyes didn't follow him. Tommy explained, "Instead, his head turned. When I went from one end of the room to the other, he turned his head again. I thought Charlie's response might be reflexive, too, so I walked back to the door, and his head turned toward the door. That was progress!"

"Okay, doctor," Tommy asked. "Can you explain this one to me? How does your head turn?"

"Well, that could be a reflex, too. We don't know." The doctor did more arm-drop tests, which Charlie passed. Eventually, the doctor admitted that maybe Charlie was getting a little better. So, they waited a few more days, after which Tommy asked a Ellis a question, "Ellis, how do we know if Charlie can't breathe on his own?"

"That's a real question. Because Charlie has the tube down his throat, the doctors must think he can't breathe on his own."

Ellis sent out an email to the chain of family members following the progress on August 1st: "By the strict interpretation of his directive, we passed the point of Do Not Resuscitate a couple of days ago. Mentally, Charlie has virtually plateaued. His eye contact is a little better, but I see no reason not to let it go a few more days to see any if there is further development." The debate on ending Charlie's life continued.

Tommy questioned removing the breathing tube: "Why don't we test it out? He's all drugged up. That is probably what's helping him stay in this coma. If you take the tube out of his throat, and he breathes on his own, maybe he'll start coming out of the coma."

Ellis said, "Yeah that's a good thing, but we can't do that because he did not want to be resuscitated. If we pull out the tube, then he either makes it or doesn't, but he won't have a chance to get better."

"Well, we can always intubate again," Tommy said.

"No, we can't because we cannot resuscitate.'"

"Well, Ellis, you have power of attorney. Tell them you're revoking the Do Not Resuscitate request, and we're going to do a test."

For the full day, Ellis and Tommy went around and round with the doctors on that point. They didn't like it. They said they just wanted to see if he can breathe on his own. Either he can or he can't. If he can't, then we can put the tube in again.

"No, you can't," they were told.

Pulling the Plug

The doctors were resistant, but honored the family's wishes after Ellis made it clear that they wanted to do it anyway.

Okay, this was it!

The doctors pulled the tube from Charlie's throat, and, to everybody's astonishment, he started breathing on his own! At first it was a big gulp! But later he started breathing regularly. He needed oxygen to keep his levels up, but he didn't need that tube stuck down his throat.

However, he was still in a coma and unresponsive. The doctor was doing all nerve tests like opening his eyes, yelling his name, and saying, "Squeeze my finger."

Charlie responded to none of it. Ellis asked the doctor again, "What do we do since there is no response?"

The doctor explained that they would give Charlie a large dose of morphine while they quit giving him food or water. The patient starves to death, but doesn't feel it because of the morphine. That is the hard reality of our choice-less choice. Moreover, it was Ellis's responsibility and his promise to Charlie that he wasn't going to leave him as a vegetable.

While Charlie's friends and family hoped and prayed for his recovery, chances were slim. Walking pneumonia had gotten so bad in his lungs that his oxygen levels dipped to the point where his brain protected itself. He had a sepsis infection when the bacteria in his blood and brain signaled the organs to shut down, except for the heart and lungs. The brain was not able to provide circulation to his hands or his legs. The brain was in a coma and Charlie wasn't conscious, in their world anyway. The neurologist explained that the brain, when faced with this type of massive challenge, insulates itself and goes into hibernation.

Ellis's biggest fear was that he would have to say, "Put

him down."

The doctors were explicit in telling Ellis that he had the responsibility to make this choice because Charlie was clear about what he wanted in his Do Not-Resuscitate document. He didn't want to be a vegetable.

As he worked with and listened to the doctors all day, Ellis was trying to figure out what was around the corner. He went to Charlie's house to see what needed to be done, filed, or fixed?

He found our mother's silver sitting in Charlie's garage in a box, so he took that to the safety deposit box. He gave Charlie's gun to his good friend, Steve Wilson. He looked for anything that someone might want to steal. He was doing for Charlie what he had donefor their mother, like making sure all bills were paid. Expensive items were safe, and the house was secure. He could trust that if Charlie lived, his home would be ready, and he did not have to worry about the daily stuff.

On the other hand, if Charlie did not make it, Ellis contacted a couple of real estate agents because that's what he did for a living. He said, "I may have a referral for you soon. My brother's not doing well." Ellis does referrals across the country all the time, so he was quickly able to identify one or two people who would have been able to sell his house for him. Then there was Charlie's car, and the family silver, and other items he set aside for family members to share, split up, or pass along to the next generation.

Ellis spent the time and went through Charlie's entire house and made two big piles. One huge pile was of things that didn't matter anymore. The other collection consisted of important papers, house deed, and bills–he organized everything. Ellis did this knowing that he was going to be Charlie's durable power of attorney and executor when that day came. Ironically, he had just called him on July 3, before he left to visit my family for the July 4 holiday. Ellis asked Charlie to bring me his list of passwords on his computer for safe-keeping. He didn't realize he was going to need them a week later. Ellis had to get into Charlie's Comcast account, his banking accounts, his website, his credit-card accounts, mortgage accounts, and such. The two or three times that he did not have a password, he could talk to someone at that company through having the durable power of attorney. Having the passwords also became a joke among the brothers like when Chris handed him an envelope and said half in jest, "Here are my passwords. So, you think I should be worried about this? You know, the last time Charlie gave his passwords to you, he was in the hospital within a week."

While Charlie was in the hospital, his brothers and Steve went to his house and did a general house cleaning. They generously described Charlie's lifestyle as a bachelor's lifestyle. When they walked into some rooms, they gasped, "Oh my God."

The kitchen needed a thorough clean-up. When they saw Charlie's microwave oven, they declared it to be an environmental hazard. In the end, Steve just tossed it and bought Charlie a new one.

In his role, he was planning the funeral because Charlie wasn't getting any better, and they expected that pulling the tube out of his throat could do it, but it didn't. Next, since

Ellis had the durable power of attorney, his responsibility was to make sure that Charlie did not get stuck in a vegetative state.

As Tommy said, "Look, he's not going anywhere. He's not dying now. So, let's just see what happens."

There was no urgency on anybody's part.

Pastor Paul

Charlie's good friend was Pastor Paul Richardson of Mariners Community Church in Half Moon Bay. He has a deep friendship with Charlie, telling Charlie's brothers, "I met Charlie around 2001. He is a larger-than-life guy with a big heart of gold. He is a sensitive soul who loves so hard and so deep because he has real compassion for people. Likewise, when he hurts, the pain is also profound. I spent time walking him through his pain on several occasions.

"As his pastor, I found him to be honest about himself and not afraid to get the support of people around him to help him. He always heard me when I said, 'You messed up there, Charlie.' We'd have a big laugh about it. He is not pretentious and hides nothing. We could have frank, open, and honest conversations. That's how our relationship began and had progressed over the years."

Pastor Paul was on vacation when he got a call that Charlie was in the hospital, and was going to die. The message was grave, and Paul was shocked! "What do you mean he is going to die? Charlie is a big, robust man, and a strong guy!" When Paul heard that Charlie was in complete organ failure, he cut his vacation short.

Paul went to visit Charlie in the hospital, and he was

saddened to see him hooked up to several machines. They were keeping him alive. When Paul saw him, that was when Paul understood the prognosis that his body shutting down. He remained comatose and not at all responsive. Paul gazed at the machines and the monitors and wondered how Charlie was truly doing in there. He prayed over him, and finally told his wife that Charlie was not going to be with them for much longer. He continued to talk to and pray with the persons who came to visit Charlie. In time, Paul finally grasped that he had to prepare for Charlie's memorial service.

Paul began to sift through his experiences with Charlie and asked himself several questions. How would I describe his character? What funny stories did he share? What fun stuff have we done? How had he inspired and supported others?

"Once when I met yours and Charlie's mother, she rendered her version of a Bible quote from John 14. She said to me in her Southern drawl: 'Jesus said, 'In my Father's house there are many mansions—I go there to prepare a place for you.' And she would say, ' am sure Charlie is going to Heaven, although his room may be somewhat Spartan!'" Paul explained to Charlie's brothers as they spoke about the pending memorial service.

"My thoughts were in preparation: I will need to say goodbye. I am going to be doing the memorial service in two weeks. What did his mom say to him about heaven? I was just honestly beginning to prepare for my goodbyes to him and dealing with my personal feelings of loss."

Conditions Persist

The question on everyone's mind became: would Charlie survive the toxic pneumococcal sepsis, which sparks the brain to defend the body by shutting down the organs? His four weeks in the intensive care unit followed his stumbling around SFO for over 24 hours. Doctors had already determined that he was going to die and induced his coma to help the brain and body cope. Yet, his condition went from bad to worse. At one moment, he seemed peacefully asleep. At another moment, he suffered thirteen minor strokes, while blood pressure was rising to a dangerous level. When organs fail, the body does not eliminate fluids, and Charlie had that flaccid doughboy appearance of the truly ill.

The medical problem remained that there was no cure for sepsis. Doctors tried to fight it with antibiotics, but nothing worked. However, the Eli Lilly Company was clinically testing one drug, Xigris. It was used only in the most toxic cases where no progress in treatment or therapy for sepsis worked. The drug was approved to be used on a clinical trial basis for which Charlie qualified. The medicine was very expensive, at $2500 per dose. Doctors gave Charlie one dose, a three-ounce bottle, every four hours for one week straight. Charlie, Roger, and other friends and family members were absolutely convinced that Xigris was one of the medical techniques that saved Charlie's life. The drug seemed to be the tipping point when Charlie's viral count dropped. Finally!

Billy Basset

Billy always had the uncanny sense that Charlie was there, and that gave him a little bit of hope. He could not have been happier when he heard the good news.

He said, "Then Charlie came to. Amazing! And he had a sense of humor so I knew for sure that Charlie was back. Charlie opened his eyes. So, if you ever doubted the existence of a higher power—don't. Charlie just wasn't finished here because he is one of the most charismatic people I know. He can walk into a room and command your attention. He is selfless and generous, and I am proud to call him my best friend."

Yes, a miracle occurred when Charlie opened his eyes, but he could not yet move them easily. Chris started turning on the television. What better stimulus for Charlie than the team he loved, the San Francisco Giants? They had returned to the World Series championship playoffs in the fall of 2011. They watched that game every other day to help Charlie make reconnections that were familiar. Chris also turned on TV Land, which aired television shows the brothers grew up with, like Bonanza or Gilligan's Island.

Charlie was still in the most intensive part of ICU while he was just starting to regain consciousness. One night there were seven people in the room. Marina and Kerri were sitting on the couch next to Charlie's bed so close together they rubbed elbows. Charlie was asleep, but he was facing their direction. Suddenly, he opened his eyes and saw Kerri, the ex-wife, and Marina, his girlfriend, sitting next to each other. Charlie's eyes were so huge with surprise, like bug eyes, that his body jerked on the hospital bed.

Kerri and Marina thought that Charlie's expression was priceless. They laughed hysterically, but this was before he could communicate. Charlie later said that he knew he was in trouble when he saw his ex-wife and his girlfriend sitting there in the same room looking at him. He thought he might have died and gone to the wrong place!

Sharing Stories

Occasionally, story-telling helped lighten the worries that the visitors shared for their brother, boyfriend, dad, and friend, Charlie. They all agreed that Bill's story would have won the humor award:

"I got sober in a stark way when I was thirty-five. In 1997, I left a relationship to go to Roger Berry's home and live on the couch of my best friend. I had one suitcase, forty dollars in my pocket, and tremendous sadness at what I had to show for my life. I left Phoenix in June 1997 and moved back to Lake Tahoe. In '98, Charlie called me and said, 'Billy, come to the conference. Roger's not going to make it this year, but I really want you to go.'

'You know Charlie, I don't have much money. I'm just waiting tables, but I can make it happen.'

'Look, I've got a cabin in Curry Village. We can pull the couch out, and you can sleep on it.'

'Okay, I'm coming.'

'Glad to hear it. And listen, whatever you do, don't leave any food in your car. Okay? The bears will break into the car.'

'Roger that, Charlie, I'm going to check that off my list!'"

Bill immediately cleaned out and wiped down his car. He did not want bears. He arrived Friday night at Charlie's cabin. They got up early on Sunday morning to go to a meeting, and as they walked up to Bill's car, he noticed the glass was broken on the passenger side door. The metal's bent out. Surely whoever broke into Bill's car stole his CD collection and stereo. Bill's anger turned his face red, and rightly so. He was biting mad and cussing as he and Charlie inspected the mess. Charlie looked at Bill, stopped for a second, and then looked down at the car floor. Suddenly Charlie spoke up, "I thought I told you to clean out your car!"

"I did, Charlie. I did?"

"Bill, you're just going to have to turn this over" Billy was livid and certain that Tweakers had broken in and stolen stuff.

"Billy, there's your CDs right there. Look."

Not only were the CDs on the floor, but Bill saw bear hair mixed into the mess all over the inside of the car. Appearances said the bear jumped up and down in the driver's seat where the ceiling was bent. But the stereo, the CDs, and Bill's luggage were intact.

The two men went to their meeting, and Bill was returning home to work, and needed plastic to cover the broken window. The guy behind the counter told him, "You know, the

Park Ranger's on his way over. He's going to write you a citation for leaving food in your car."

Bill went outside to his car to leave. Getting a ticket would be trouble, so he said to the Park Ranger, "There was no food in my car."

"Well, if there wasn't, there wouldn't have been a bear in your car."

Obviously, no one believed that Bill had cleaned his car thoroughly. Under the circumstances, he might not have believed it himself. He drove out of the parking lot, away from the Park Ranger, clipping along Highway 49 through Placerville and on to Lake Tahoe. Along the way, he stopped at a Wash-n-Vac to vacuum his car. Out came the glass and the bear hair until the nozzle got stuck under the back seat. There he found an apple. How? What had happened?

The week before Bill went to Yosemite, he had visited Apple Hill right outside of Placerville, California. Since it was fall, there had been fresh apples and pears for sale. Bill bought a box of fruit, and the bear smelled the one apple that lodged under the backseat. Bill called Charlie and told him the story so they could have a good laugh.

Kerri Shares

The next morning, Kerri dropped Kian and Kyla at their events. They were still sad that they had said goodbye to Charlie. Then, she went to the hospital to find out whether or not they'd pulled the plug.

She walked into the hospital room, and there were his

two brothers. At the exact moment, they both looked up at her with big eyes and smiles and never said a word.

Kerri looked at Charlie, who had no respirator, and he was breathing on his own.

"How long?" Kerri asked his brothers.

"It's been about two hours. Charlie has been breathing on his own for two hours."

"Awesome! That changes everything, right?"

Thus, they started the process of recovery, if there was to be one. At one point, when Kyla was visiting, Charlie saw her. Without any of his words, his eyes followed her, and his head turned to follow her movement.

Kyla walked into the hospital room, and she would swear that his eyes followed her across when she set my stuff down. She approached the bed and saw that his eyes were open. "Mom, I can see the pupils follow me around the room!" She could see his eyes were alert and focused on her as she walked around that room.

Chris was there communicating with Charlie by holding up a sign with a question. Verbal communication was mostly absent because he couldn't move. Charlie had been in a coma for almost six weeks. Would he recover? No one knew if he was going to be in a nursing home for the rest of his life or if he would come back fully.

The next time Kerri and the twins returned to the hospital, they found out that Charlie could talk a little bit. He told us that he heard Kyla crying. Charlie had heard her crying that night when she said goodbye. He felt she was in danger, and he needed to come back, find out what was going on, and help her.

Charlie was coming back slowly, and he thought mostly about Kyla. When Kyla visited, he would sit up and watch her. He was very animated when he was looking at her.

Tommy's Second Visit

Tommy returned to be with Ellis and Charlie for the next week. When he went to California a second time, he saw that Charlie's eyes did follow him around the room. The occasions seemed rare, and he wondered: Maybe his eyes are just following objects. But then he observed Charlie's vital signs improving. The doctor was going to move him to the ICU step-down, which was the best news.

When Charlie tried to talk, Tommy felt assured that his condition was improving. On the day when they moved him to ICU step-down, the attendants removed him from the gurney, and they bumped him hard down on the bed, and Tommy heard him say, "Dammit!"

"What an excellent sound! Charlie was back!" Tommy declared.

Chris was the steady communicator in helping Charlie express himself. Over the next several days, Charlie's progression seemed a little steadier. The doctors still monitored Charlie for MSRA, and Chris didn't want to sit with his face right in Charlie's face trying to listen to what he was saying. Then, a doctor gave him a stethoscope which he held next to Charlie's mouth as he was trying to talk. Chris heard part of what he whispered, but it was still a bit scratchy. And then later the doctors also used the stethoscope to listen to Charlie's responses.

Chris had some notepads and pens so Charlie and I could communicate through writing.

Where am I? Charlie asked.

Chris wrote the word "Hospital" on a large pad, and then wrote "Pneumonia, getting better."

Chris asked, "Who am I? Tommy, Chris, or Ellis?" He pointed to each name, yet Charlie didn't respond. He didn't know who I was yet, but he's at least aware of himself. Several days had passed before Charlie knew who I was and could point out other people's names, too.

Charlie graduated from the University of Arkansas, and when the Arkansas basketball game was on the television, he recognized his team. They continued with identifying those small things through Charlie's response to Chris's 'blink twice.' Chris would blink twice, and then Charlie would do so. The communication was starting. ■

14. Moving to Step Down

From Charlie's perspective, waking up and feeling his body was a groggy moment. Questions swirled: Where am I? What happened? Why can't I move?

Years later, when he speaks about his experience, he tells people, "When I woke up around August fourth, I was barely able to respond. Yet three days later, I was able to wiggle one finger. By August eighth, I was able to mouth the words 'I'm thirsty' and I could wiggle my feet and my fingers on request. Actually, that was exceptional progress for an atrophied body that was bed-ridden for six weeks."

After coming out of the coma, and as Charlie progressed, he was moved out of ICU to the next level down, which is called step-down care. The main difference between the levels of care was the monitoring. In ICU, medical staff monitored Charlie around the clock. In step-down care, he was monitored every few hours. While that was supposed to be positive, Charlie had a real problem of being totally dehydrated. He was dying of thirst.

His body was so dehydrated and starved for water that his brain was plotting a solution. Remember, he could not move much at all. He was to barely able to wiggle fingers and toes and couldn't speak beyond a whisper. Nurses walked by his room at all hours, day and night, and he tried to call them, "Help. I'm so thirsty. Help please?" Nobody could hear him. In fact, he could barely hear himself.

He was staring above his bedpost where there was a two-gallon container of what looked like chocolate milk. He followed the feeding tube that hooked from his nose into the container of his chocolate milk fantasy—nutritious, delicious, sweet chocolate milk soothing his parched throat. He became fixated on that two-gallon container. He hatched a detailed plan of how he was going to get to it. First, he would move his arm over to the rail of the bed. Next, he would pull himself up to a sitting position. He would get that container of chocolate milk and chug it down! He was so thirsty. The problem was he couldn't move his arm to get to the rail of the bed to move anything. Bummer. That was probably the longest four hours of his life, trying to will, move, or project his arm to over to the bed rail.

Finally, a male nurse came by to check on Charlie, who whispered, "Help. I'm thirsty I'm thirsty."

This nurse was on the night shift, and said, "Well we can't really give you any water. We can give you ice chips that you can suck." As he talked closely so Charlie could hear him, the overwhelming odor of alcohol from his breath caused Charlie to try and back away. Well, the last thing Charlie needed was to get drunk off this guy's smell. However, the nurse gave him some ice chips, and later on, he brought water and nourishment.

The ninth of August brought more recovery of skills. Charlie was starting to be able to communicate and Chris was using sign language and writing answers for Charlie on a large piece of tablet paper. In a whisper, Charlie mouthed questions like...

"Where am I?"

In the hospital!

"What happened?"

You got pneumonia and sepsis.

"How long?"

Going on five weeks.

Charlie and Chris progressed accordingly in helping him reconnect the new information in his brain and learn what the next steps would be. Because Charlie could just whisper, Chris would place the stethoscope next to his mouth and listen to my requests like "Where's Kyla?"

Chris called Kyla, who came bouncing into the room all full of smiles.

"What was wrong, Kyla?" Charlie asked, remembering her crying.

At first, she was confused, but eventually she got it, and gave two-thumbs up and answered, "It's all good Dad, I'm fine!"

Charlie relied on his friends, children, and brothers to hear him and to respond until he gained enough of his strength and movement back.

Charlie remained in the step-down nursing level for about one week before being moved into skilled nursing, which is like the regular hospital. He liked the regular hospital because it was brand new and had all the latest, state-of-the-art equipment. He could watch television, especially the San Francisco Giants because of the season pennant run at the end of the season. Their pitcher was a really good closer for the Giants. Also, Ellis and Chris had him watching childhood shows of the 1960s and '70s. They wanted to spark memories, and Charlie did react positively.

Charlie was first introduced to a Greek doctor, Dr. Aftonomous, who started coming by every other day to check on his progress. He asked Charlie questions like who was President of the United States and what month was it? Also, Charlie sensed he was trying to softly persuade him to utilize the hospital services when it came time to move out of the skilled nursing area and go into focus rehabilitation. The visitors who came to see him next were the professionals with whom he would be working. The physical therapist was Natalie. Laurie was the occupational therapist.

Dr. A, as he was called, asked Charlie how he got to San Francisco. Charlie said, "I had a weird recollection, but give me a few days to separate the fantasy from the reality."

A few days later he came by and asked Charlie again how he got to San Francisco. This time Charlie was certain. He told him when he had missed his flight in Atlanta and had found some Saudi Arabian sheiks, whom he paid $20,000 to take him to San Francisco on their private Lear jet. On the trip, he noticed they had AK-47 rifles, and when asked, they told him they had diplomatic immunity, as they were bodyguards for the Prince.

Dr. A looked over to Ellis and asked, "Is this true?"

Ellis said, "No. He got on the next Delta flight."

Now Charlie was the one who was really confused. He believed his story. What they determined later, after connecting the dots, was that everyone was encouraged to talk with him while he was comatose because no one knew what he could hear or recognize. It turned out that Tommy happened to be speaking on the phone with a Saudi Prince, and asked Charlie if he wanted to speak with him. Charlie's eyes had been partially opened, and he saw the medical equipment and monitoring devices. He misconstrued those to be the cockpit of a Lear Jet. Therefore, the illusion of that story was born in his mind.

It took a while to separate what was fantasy from reality, especially with the intense drugs that were in his system, but the spiritual experience remained intact. He desperately wanted to stay on the morphine because he had never experienced this unprecedented level of pain.

He explained to the doctor that he was easily addicted and the time would come when he would need to wean him off of the morphine. Yet, at the current moment, the medication did relieve the pain, anxiety, and probably even depression after what he had experienced. Dr. A assured Charlie not to worry, that when the day came, they would wean him off the medication. However, when that day came, the addict in him asked if we could just wait one more day!

Charlie also continued to be dehydrated, and getting something to drink was his constant quest. He could not get enough liquids. When the time came that his throat muscles worked, and he could swallow, they gave him a cup of apple juice. Charlie called it the nectar of the gods because it was so refreshing. He needed as much liquid nourishment as his body could now handle the swallowing, digestion, and elimination. He didn't want to appear as the dough boy any more.

Charlie's brothers volunteered to start his physical therapy slowly to move him forward and eliminate the hospital's liability concerns. They were taught and did the exercises where they would lift Charlie's arm, move it, rotate it, and return it to the bed because he wasn't able to do it by himself. Exercises like this continued until August 24th, when the doctor said, "Okay, you need to make a decision to move into focus rehab."

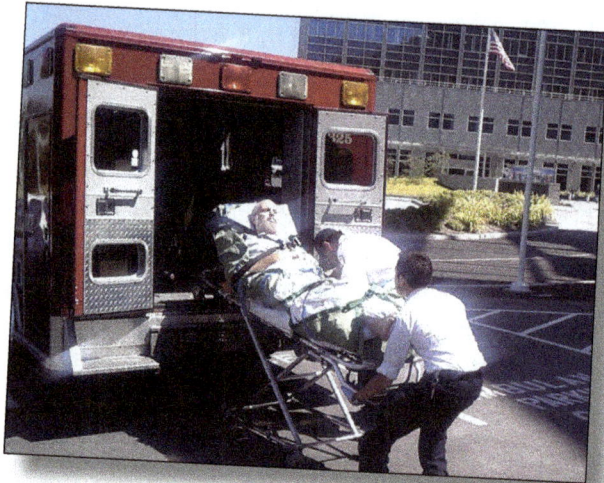

'Going down" to focused rehab ■

Charlie went with Dr. Aftonomous because the rehabilitation center was right down the street from the hospital. They wanted to move him that day, and his intuition perked up. He explained to the doctors that he was going to wait until his brother Ellis, who had the power of attorney, returned from Tennessee.

When the hospital explained that were going to move Charlie, and that his insurance would not cover any more hospital pay, he said the word 'no' more firmly. He took action. Charlie sent a message to Steve and Ellis to contact the hospital as his lawyer. "Tell them I'm not being moved until one of you two arrives."

Steve is a lawyer who works for one of the oldest law firms in San Francisco, and he was able to write a very legal looking letter informing the hospital that the patient is not going to be moved until his brother is present. The hospital suddenly complied and became willing to wait the extra day. Ellis arrived, as did moving day. An ambulance carried Charlie down the hill to the rehabilitation center. Ellis sent an email out to the group because by this time they've been communicating for several months about Charlie's progress. Ellis's message was: Charlie is going down. Of course, everybody on the lists responds with

My God what happened?

Oh no. we are so sorry?

What happened? Did he take a turn for the worse?

Then Ellis sent out his second email, rephrasing his words. "He's going down the hill to focus rehab." People on the list were grateful that he clarified that fact.

Now it was time for Laurie, the occupational therapist and Natalie, the physical therapist to work with Charlie. They helped save his life because it was their jobs to give him the exercise to become fully functional again. For example, Laurie started teaching Charlie how to brush his teeth. Yes, he was taking baby steps, but he was overjoyed to be learning and healing.

Of course, the stint in rehabilitation had its less-than-finer moments. The personnel came to check his vitals every three hours, like clockwork, all day and all night. They were bugging Charlie, who could not sleep. Lack of sleep caused him to be irritated. He finally said to the doctor, "Look, nurses are still coming in day and night. I need sleep time. I need to be left alone at night. Unless it is a life-threatening situation, I need to sleep at night."

Then, sure enough, at 2 am, two attendants arrived. Charlie told them he wanted to be left alone. They responded with telling him they needed to weigh him.

"At 2 o'clock in the morning?" He was beyond irate. "You guys are going to mess around here taking blood pressure and dilly dally, and you won't be out of here until five ." They said they would be quick, but Charlie knew they wouldn't be.

The techs took his weight, and although the bed Charlie was in had an automatic weight reading, they were not satisfied with that. They hooked him up in this big bag and lifted him up in an A-frame, which actually cracked his back, which felt pretty good. They pulled him up in this sack to get his weight, starting at just after 2 o'clock in the morning. By the time they got through fiddling around and they were leaving, Charlie called to them, "Hey guys, what time is it?"

"Uhhh, 5 am."

"Gee. Imagine that."

When the doctor came in the next day, Charlie asked that he put a Do Not Disturb note on the door at night. The doctor complied, and Charlie started getting some rest.

The regiment of physical therapy by that time was all small steps: leg lifting, knee bending, wiggling toes, sticking his tongue out. These rudimentary steps led to bigger advances: sitting up, pulling legs over the bed, and rotating. Natalie helped Charlie sit up because he was still getting visitors. The day came when it was time to stand up. Charlie had a couple of visitors, George Muteff and Freda Jeffs, from his local community. They updated him on the latest local and political gossip. While they were chatting, Natalie came in to exercise him while he was standing. Natalie pulled around a walker and explained the steps.

"You are going to sit up like you've been practicing.

Then, you are going to put your arms up and on the walker, and I'm going to help you rock up to standing on your feet."

As if Charlie needed any motivation, Natalie was a well-endowed woman. When she bent over to coax him into standing up, he had a lot of motivation to rock up, then stand up and balance on his feet. She was a good sport and took his flirting in stride. Around September 1st when Charlie could actually walk a little bit, he had achieved a big milestone that got emailed to the group: I was able to walk 47 steps today. Believe me, it was huge deal that Natalie would take me slowly on my daily walks, and eventually I made it all the way down to the rehab workout center where I could get on the bicycle for a few minutes. That offered me another type of exercise. Other exercises included throwing a bean bag into the bean bag hole. I am making good progress.

In the meantime, Charlie's recovery friends brought

meetings into focus rehab, and he could move the wheelchair into the outdoor area and get some sun and fresh air. It was all part of the recovery process. Then, as rehab came to a close, Laurie was kind of taking over by putting the walker in front of him and he rocked to a standing position on his own to move to the bathroom. She gave him a toothbrush and coached him through the steps, and such rudimentary tasks were slowly returning his skills.

Charlie's weeks of beard growth truly qualified him as the wild man of the Smokey Mountains. His longer hair was unkempt, and they helped him shellac it black like the San Francisco Giants pitcher, Brian Wilson, who put boot polish on his beard to make it really black. The therapists found unusual ways to have some fun while retraining skills. Then again, Laurie had to show Charlie how to take a shower, which was a little embarrassing.

Finally, it was time to go home. ■

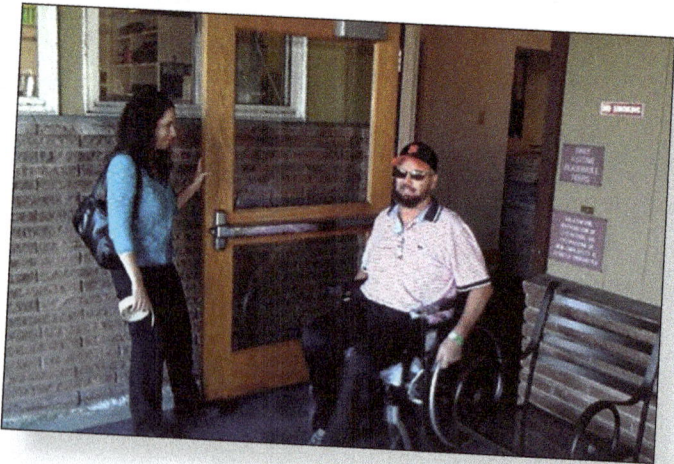

Charlie brought out at Focused Rehab ■

15. Recovering with Much Help

"Here on earth you will have many trials and sorrows. But take heart, because I have overcome the world"
—Jesus in John 16:33 NLT

Laurie and Natalie, the two therapists who helped Charlie, went to his house and inspected it to ensure that he had adequate access. Some local contractor buddies and personal friends of Charlie poured concrete and made ramps so they could push him in the wheelchair up and around to the back of his house. The front of the house is on a slope with a hill, and the only access was to climb the stairs. The second path led to the back entrance, which was through his bedroom. Laurie and Natalie approved the transfer plan. What a huge series of events took place to strap Charlie into the car, then put him in the wheelchair and wheel him around back into the bedroom. To be home was a relief and also exhausting, Charlie flopped down on the bed and slept for about 6 hours.

He was home!

He was alive!

He was grateful.

For the first month or so, people were at the house to help him readjust, keep up with his therapies, and learn to maneuver around. Chris, and then Roger stayed, and Charlie became more functional each day, which was wonderful. He could get up and go to the bathroom or make it into the living room and flop on the couch. Mostly in that first month, he slept and drank apple juice. He gradually went from eating a little to inhaling the hot food brought once a day by the women of Mariner's Community Church in Half Moon Bay. They were warm-hearted people helping people like others did in the first century of Christianity. Like most proud men, it was often easy for Charlie to be giving, and sometimes, it was not so easy for him to receive. He learned about humility and gratitude during this period.

He worked with a speech therapist to enunciate, and strengthen the vocal chords. They worked on chewing, swallowing, and moving the tongue and neck. Psychological tests would determine if strokes and subsequent experiences caused brain damage. He passed all those tests. When he first entered the ICU, he was the fifth patient to have sepsis at that time. He was the only patient with sepsis to leave the hospital alive. A curious event happened on the October day that the hospital released him to go home. The manufacturer, Eli Lilly, took Xigris off the market. Is that not an irony, or perhaps a miracle? To date, there is no known treatment which cures sepsis, and that is partially due to the high cost of research.

Much time passed after Charlie opened his eyes and became capable of moving and improving his condition. Neither his doctors nor his friends had a way to gauge his capabilities. Yet, his friends called it a miracle that he returned to normal functioning. At the same time, Charlie had become a different person. He was more involved at an intimate level with the twins, like showing up in a wheelchair for his children's water-polo games and being more involved overall. He started to look at life differently, too. For example, he was very driven at work, and he still worked hard. However, he also developed an interest in other endeavors, like personal relationships, traveling, and church activities. The twins and Kerri were so happy he was still around, and she considered him a good friend. They could talk with each other and solve whatever problems might be up for discussion.

What Kerri learned from this experience was not to rush the judgments and decisions to pull the plug so quickly. Miracles do happen.

Maureen McGlaughlin, told his brothers, "I know Charlie through a support group for recovery and because he is my neighbor in a very small community. I discovered he was in the hospital from other support group members, but I have also been a nurse for forty-five years, so I knew what was going on. If you have septic pneumonia you usually die from it."

Maureen also knew Kerri for over twenty years, and when she visited Charlie in the hospital, she connected with the family. During her many years of nursing, she had seen people recover from seemingly hopeless situations. When she first saw Charlie, she couldn't help but think how bad the situation was, and he had been hospitalized for only a day or two. Clinically speaking, the longer Charlie was in ICU and whether he remained on a respirator, the worse the progno-sis would be. Since Maureen already knew Kerri from before she became pregnant with the twins, and had watched them grow up, she wanted to offer support and be there to talk with them. She was in ICU as a visitor for Kerri and the twins mostly. Maureen would greet them by putting her arms around the kids. She hugged them both and gave them a kiss to soothe their grieving, as she knew they loved their dad dearly. Their tears were heartbreaking. Maureen was also able to be there at times during Charlie's recovery. Having seen other people go through this, the process is frequently slow, individualized, and methodical. Little movements will come back first in his activities of daily living, like going to the restroom and feeding himself. However, the patient's will is important. Charlie was a strong believer, and his faith carried him through the endeavors. He knew that faith can move mountains, and when he came back, he had a very strong, iron-clad resolve that he was saved from this impending death for a reason. He came back with an attitude like every day is a good one. He felt he was saved for a reason and looked at how he could help others, and that has been his nature anyway.

Starting Over Again

Charlie's family and friendships would sustain him emotionally over the long run. He had to retrain his body all over again, from walking to taking a bite and learning to chew and swallow. The challenge of returning to normal seemed very far away to Charlie. In fact, he had to ask himself if this state was now his new normal. His brother Ellis had resigned him from the School Board, and later told Charlie he almost resigned him from his job at Kiewit. Charlie told his younger brother that if Ellis did that, Charlie would come back from wherever he was to haunt him!

Once, very soon after returning home from the hospital, Charlie and Roger were having dinner when a piece of meat stuck in Charlie's throat, and he had to go back to emergency room for an endoscopy to clear the esophagus. Roger was with Charlie when the doctor admitted him and kept him overnight.

His muscles were weak from lack of use in the hospital. The esophagus was long and slender, and even a small piece of meat could cause this choking problem. To Charlie, this felt like a panic attack in which breathing was a difficult effort, and the body gasped for oxygen. Nothing would go down, or come up, and the only way to clear it was to poke it through. This happened three times after Charlie came home from the hospital.

When Roger accompanied to the hospital for the third time, the doctor first had to put him under to perform the endoscopy. Charlie then developed atrial fibrillation, which is an irregular heartbeat. To avoid the chances of having a stroke, the doctor put him on Warfarin, a blood thinner, but to have an endoscopy while on blood thinner was dangerous. They were about to put Charlie under to have the endoscopy when he spoke up with concern, "Doc, you know I am on Warfarin, right?"

"Really? When was the last time you were tested?"

"Two-thirty in the morning when I came in."

"What did you test at?"

"Six-point-one."

"Oh God, we can't go in! You'll bleed. You'll die."

"Yes, that's what I am telling you. Don't you have it on your notes? In my medical records? I was just in here."

The doctor went so far as to admit Charlie officially into the hospital again, and he was ready to try again by giving Charlie vitamin K to get the blood to the right thickness at 1.0 or at least below a 2.0. However, that was not working.

The doctor said, "Well, we need to go in there." By now, Charlie had a large piece of meat lodged right in the valve of his stomach. "When we go in, we are going to put you on plasma. That will make you get to the numbers that you want." They ordered three units of plasma, and they started the first drip. Roger had delayed a flight to Phoenix and stayed with Charlie at the hospital.

However, Charlie said to Roger, "Look, go back to Phoenix, and call me when you get to the airport, and call me again when you get home. It seems to be going okay right now, and I've got somebody coming to pick me up afterwards. Thanks for coming. I'll see you later."

As Charlie requested, Roger called him when he got to the airport, and by that time Charlie was having new symptoms. "Roger, I am itching like crazy, and the nurse came in to check on me, and what she saw made her panic."

Charlie was red from the enormous hives that started to spread from his chest as burning sensations down his entire body. The itching was not bearable. The physician gave Charlie the wrong blood type, which caused the staff to panic and go into a frenzy mode of operation.

"We've got to cut it off. Stop it. Get him ready for

ICU."

The reaction was so intense as to be unbearable. Charlie said, "No! I will not go back into the ICU. If I went there, I would not make it out. You've got to fix this, and you've got to fix this now."

The doctor came up to Charlie, trying to calm him down. "We'll give you some Benadryl. We're going to get this corrected. Calm down." The doctor did take care of the situation. This was one more visit of several that Charlie would have over the next year. He became a regular.

Help Continued

Charlie's brothers were coming out to help him on a regular, rotating basis. Roger, Bill, Tom and Lisa Hanley, Steve, and church members also gave support. One most important member of Charlie's networking team was Joan Madsen, his massage therapist. Charlie met Joan when she joined his chiropractor's practice. One day, when she overheard the chiropractor's wife talking to a patient about Charlie being on his death bed, her ears perked up at the phrase "pull the plug."

Joan's mouth dropped open at learning the conversation was about Charlie. Her hands that massaged and healed were needed for Charlie's recovery. The wife gave Joan the phone numbers she had for a few of Charlie's friends, but no one was returning Joan's calls. She knew first-hand how reducing stress and learning to accept being touched again after six weeks in a hospital bed would speed Charlie's health.

If there was any assistance Joan could offer, she would help Charlie.

Finally, Joan called the hospital and Charlie's son, Kian, answered the phone.

"Hello," said Joan, "I am Charlie's masseuse." That was all she had to say.

"Do you want to see him?"

"Yes."

"He wants to see you, too."

Joan jumped in her car and drove the forty-minutes to Mills-Peninsula Hospital. She had no idea what she'd encounter in the ICU. She walked into Charlie's room and thought he looked like a steamroller had flattened him. His arms laid at his sides because he couldn't move anything, not even his fingers. He had also lost the use of his legs, and was down over 100 pounds from the severity of the sepsis infection.

Charlie had turned his head towards Joan's entrance and his eyes seemed full of 200% Charlie. She wanted to try to help him improve and come all the way back. She felt his fully alive eyes told the story better than his body, which was not functioning yet.

Joan asked Charlie, "What do you want me to do?" She leaned very close to hear Charlie's whispered response, "Head." Joan got behind the head of hospital bed and massaged to ease the tightness from Charlie's head, neck, and shoulders. As she continued to return every day, she invigorated the circulation in his arms and legs. Joan returned each day for several months to help Charlie's body maintain circulation, relaxation, and healing. As time went on, Joan witnessed Charlie move a finger and eventually develop greater range of movement in his hands and arms and other extremities.

A rumor travelled quickly along the hospital ward that some rich guy in room 1080 has his own private masseuse coming in each day to massage him. What no one knew was that Joan was doing it for free since Charlie didn't know where he stood financially.

The nurses attending Charlie grew concerned and asked Joan to stop massaging him. They feared that massage could loosen a blood clot, which Joan didn't believe. After that, Joan consulted with the doctors and explained her technique, and they permitted her to proceed. As a result, Joan was present each day to witness the miracle of Charlie's step-by-step return, especially when he sat up. That was such excellent progress surpassed only by his finally standing upright on his own.

Welcome Home Party

Charlie's manager from Kiewit had hung a huge banner they had made that said, "Welcome Home, Charlie!" They had shipped from Maryland some blue crab with chunks of meat and crab cakes wrapped in individual containers. The celebration of Charlie returning home was on!

Also, his boss at Kiewit had marshaled all of the superintendents to bring their barbecue gear, like the 55-gallon drum. They grilled tri-tip steaks, hamburgers, and hotdogs.

They had invited all of Charlie's friends, and the members of the school board. Even the school superintendent celebrated.

Everyone who came to Charlie's homecoming party shared the same joy that he was home finally. Charlie circled around the house in his wheelchair. He was wheeling himself around with his feet and not using the hands on the wheels. He looked so happy greeting friends and receiving congratulations for being alive.

Kyla, Roger, Kerri and School Supt. Gaskill at the Welcome Home party

Oct. 25, 2011
■

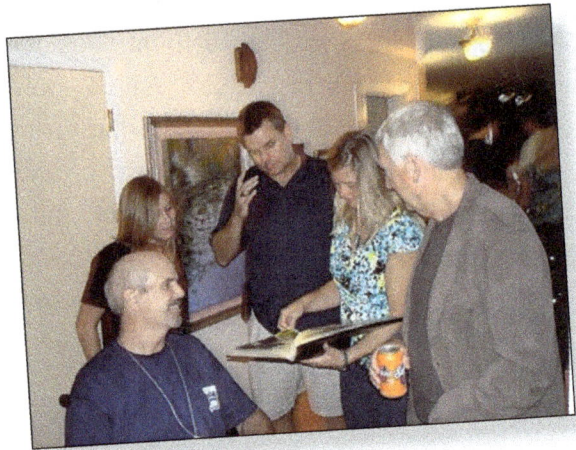

The house overflowed with people who were gathered to celebrate life. Charlie was reminded how nothing ever gets him down, and how much he shines with friends and family members. He was having a good time being home. For him, he was happy that he was home because he could continue his therapeutic massage.

Joan continued working on him several times a week until Charlie went back to work in January. The company had saved his position throughout his illness. In the beginning,

Charlie was only able to stay half a day for two days. Then he worked for three half-days a week as his focus improved. He just kept building himself back up. Joan helped ease the neuropathy in his hands and feet. For a while, Charlie insisted that he attend the Yosemite Conference, but he became sick in the change of altitude. He also started putting on weight, which the body does to protect itself after trauma.

Generous Help and Support

Ellis is a methodical person by nature, which helped Charlie tremendously. He asked Ellis at one point where he was financially. Weeks had passed and he was home recovering, but he was worried. He had this house. He had a house up in Tahoe, which was a vacation rental with contracts, bills, and management tasks.

Ellis calmly told him, "Yes, I've taken care of everything. I think you owe the house cleaner in Tahoe three hundred dollars. Other than that, you are current."

"Current? That's great. Ellis, you've taken such great, professional care of my finances." Ellis took the time, spending long hours sorting through all of Charlie's paper piles, stocks, housewares, and everything eventually. Ellis knew he would be the one to dispose of Charlie's stuff if he had passed away. Ellis would sell the house, prepare it for sale, as he did with their mom's home. Ellis had all of Charlie's insurance notifications and medical claims, which looked to be over a foot thick. He managed all those details.

Recovery Seems S-L-O-W

Otherwise Charlie's recovery became monotonous. He settled in and watched every television episode of The Sopranos and every Big Bang Theory episode. In several episodes in the Sopranos (Season 6, Episodes 2 &3), Tony Soprano had the same experience as Charlie did with Sepsis, even down to the part where his daughter called him back as he was crossing over. Charlie sat in tears watching both episodes, and got a sense of how traumatic it had to be for the friends and family members. He also had a lot of time to think through that his brothers and my friends didn't experience what he had. He slept through it while they lived each day waiting for him to die, praying that he wouldn't. They were preparing for his death while celebrating their families and connections. What they lived through was not fun. Charlie was happy, even thrilled, that now the worst was behind them. Or so he thought.

Ellis left Charlie with a tall stack of papers to go through. Charlie noticed on one medical document, that was early in the process of his medical emergency, that doctors had diagnosed him with bone cancer, Osteosarcoma. Since their dad died of bone cancer, Charlie picked up the phone and called Ellis.

"Hey Ellis, I found a paper in that stack you left for me. I see that I was diagnosed with bone cancer. Remember Dad died of that, and I have it?"

"Well, that did come up, but remember Charlie we were trying to keep you alive at the time. It didn't seem as such a big deal since you were going through so much already. Maybe you should call Chris. I think he knows more about it."

When Charlie called Chris next, he said, "I'm going through these papers and it shows that they diagnosed me with bone cancer. Remember Dad died of bone cancer. Ellis said you knew more about what was going on then."

"Oh yeah, they said that the test was positive for that, but you know they didn't make a big deal of it. The sepsis was more critical at the time because, Charlie, remember they were trying to keep you alive. Maybe you should call your neurologist Dr. Steyer. He was the guy who made the diagnosis."

Charlie's call to Dr. Steyer elicited his return call about one hour later. When Charlie explained his concern, the doctor said he would review the records. He explained, "We did have a positive test result, but it was somewhat inconclusive. You must remember, though," Charlie broke in, "I know, I know, you were trying to save my life" Dr. Steyer continued, "What I would suggest is scheduling an MRI if you are able to get out and about."

Luckily, Charlie had just learned how to drive again and could get to the hospital by himself. He was nervous, even scared. He had just barely survived. Then to come home and find out he had bone cancer and was likely going to die anyway was a lot to handle. To quiet that voice, he had an MRI, during which they had to inject him with a dye that makes your bones turn blue. The time it takes for the bones to turn blue is two hours, and the doctor can see every aspect of the bones.

When the nurse injected the dye, Charlie asked, "Has anyone ever had a negative reaction to the injections?" He was feeling queasy at the same time the nurse explained the mixture was composed of water and a little bit of nuclear dye and nobody ever...

Charlie heard no more because he fainted, fell forward and smashed his face on the linoleum floor. The nurse patted his cheeks and called his name until he came to again. They put him on a gurney and rolled once again into the emergency room. The clinician stopped at the desk to ask where room #4 was, to which Charlie said, "It's right over there, I've been there a bunch of times!"

One nurse welcomed him with, "Hey Mr. Gardner, you're back. What is it? Your esophagus?"

"Nope, a bone cancer scare this time!" he explained.

By now, Charlie's patience was worn very thin, as all he wanted to know was whether or not he had bone cancer. They officially, finally completed the MRI, and because the day was Friday, they said the results would be sometime during the next week. "But don't worry. Your doctor will call you."

"That's not going to happen," Charlie started. "I'm not going to sit around all week and wonder if I have bone cancer."

Charlie went proactive and called his primary physician, Pamela, and left a message, "I don't care what time it is when you get the results of the bone scan. You call me back."

At 11 o'clock at night, Pamela called, "Yep, the results are back. You don't have bone cancer. Unfortunately, you're going to live a lot longer." Charlie had to admire her not-so-subtle humor.

Bob Alaimo

Bob Alaimo was a special man. I say "was", because he is no longer among the living, but he is still with us. He was a living miracle, and his spirit lives on in the Coastside of Half Moon Bay California. We had a special experience together which was supernatural, but I get the sense that these were normal occurrences for Bob. But first, let me tell you a little bit about Bob.

I met Bob when I first moved to the Coastside and immediately respected how he carried himself. Bob was an ex-bouncer in a tough biker bar, looked like "Mr. Clean" with a shaved head and a handlebar moustache. His nickname was "Mad Dog". Definitely not the kind of guy you would want to mess with upon first look. But Bob was probably the kindest, gentlest man I've ever met. He was a walking Big Book in recovery, and sponsored many men. He helped a lot of people on the Coastside and made a difference in a lot of lives.

I got to know Bob well by seeing him around town and we attended a lot of the same recovery meetings. He would often quote 12 step literature and how it relates to everyday life. He and his wife, Loralyn became good friends with Kerri and I and spent time together with our kids. They came to our wedding in Yosemite, and some of my favorite memories are pictures of our kids when they were 5-6 and so innocent having fun in God's natural paradise.

One day, in 2001 while Kerri, the twins, and I were living in Arroyo Grande, we got a phone call that Bob had been in an accident. He had been playing tag football on Ocean Beach in San Francisco and went to catch a pass, got tied up with the defenseman going for the ball, and hit the deck hard. Bob recalled that as soon as he hit he knew he had extensive damage to his spinal cord, and was paralyzed from the neck down. Bob said he immediately did the first 3 steps, knowing he was powerless over his situation, and immediately came to believe that his need for God was great in this situation. The players huddled together and did the 3rd step prayer together as they awaited the ambulance. They said "God, I offer myself to thee, to build with me, and do with me as thou will. Relieve me of the bondage of self, that I may better do thy will. Take away my difficulties, that victory over them may bear witness to those I would help of thy power, thy love, and thy way of life. May I do thy will always".

Kerri and I dropped everything and drove the 4 hours up to the Bay Area and went to see Bob in the Hospital in San Mateo. Upon entering the room, it was surreal to see our good friend in his paralyzed state. The first thing that out of his mouth, he whispered, "How can I help you?" Classic Bob. Thinking of others as we were crazy worried about him. The Doctors told us that because of the extent of the damage to Bob's spinal cord, the odds were he would never recover, move his limbs, or walk again.

It wasn't long before we got a call that Bob moved.

Bob was determined to do everything he could to walk again. By the time Kerri and I returned to the Coastside in 2002, some of the men that Bob sponsored were local contractors and had made major modifications to Bob and Loralyn's house so the now wheelchair bound Bob could get around. It was a testimony to the effect Bob had on his community that these men would donate their time, energy, and money to make what would normally be a very expensive upgrade.

By a miracle, Bob learned to walk again. We were collectively worried when Bob started showing up to meetings by driving himself! But he did. That was the determination that was Bob. But it wasn't over.

By 2009, he was diagnosed with Crone's disease which is a gastrointestinal disorder, and on top of that, Bob started to show early signs of Alzheimer's disease. I'm sure he had his moments, but he insisted in continuing to carry the message and help others. He would often be heard quoting "Nothing so much insures immunity from drinking than intensive work with others.", and "The 12 steps are a spiritual group of principles, which if practiced (he would emphasize 'practice') as a way of life can expel the obsession to drink, and enable the sufferer to live happy, and usefully whole." However, Bob continued to deteriorate.

When I got sick in 2011 and was finally able to make it home, we would have meetings in my house since I wasn't very mobile as it was my turn to relearn everything. Bob was able to make it as he was living only a couple of blocks away, and the meeting soon became known as the "Bob and Charlie ain't dead yet!" meeting, and it continued for 5 years.

Bob didn't make it 5 years. He was going down as I was coming back. It was early in 2012 and I was just barely back to work. My employer was great in that they appreciated what I had to offer and I was instructed to work until I got tired and then go home. It was not unusual for me to leave early, but one day, a revelation came to me as if an angel was whispering in my ear, "Go see Bob. Go see Bob now!"

So I did. I got up, and walked out of the office telling the receptionist "I'll be back tomorrow", and then I realized I didn't know where Bob was! I called a buddy, Nate, who said he thought he was at Stanford Hospital but didn't know what room. He said he would find out and call me back, so I headed toward the Hospital. Nate called back in a few minutes and told me he was in C Ward, and gave me the room number.

I found my way there, parked, and navigated to the C Ward. Upon entering the floor, I saw Loralyn backing out of the room. She turned and exclaimed, "Charlie! Thank God you are here! I just told Bob it's OK to Go and you are exactly who he needs to see right now." Dazed, I walked into the room and saw the shell of a man I once knew. The burly, biker bar bouncer was pale, and shaking. Literally scared to death. "Bob" I said, "Good to see you brother". "Good to see you too, Charlie". "How are you doing?" I asked. "Not too good", he answered.

"Let me say, I know exactly how you feel, not long ago, I was right where you are now. You're pretty scared right now, aren't you? Bob nodded. I asked him, "Are you seeing any beings? Angels cloaked in white?" He said, "Yes, there are two here with me trying to tell me not to worry, that they are here to take me someplace."

"Those are Angels Bob, they are your spirit guides, and they are telling you to Fear Not, as Angels always do. Let me tell you from my own experience, that real soon you are going to be in a place where there is no pain, only peace and warmth. Being a believer in Christ, you are going to Heaven, and let me tell you it is a wonderful place. I can also say that I will be there with you in just the blink of an eye. It may be a while I'm still here, but it will be no time at all that I join you on that side of the veil." I could see Bob visibly relax. He heard and believed what I was telling him. He said, "I love you, Charlie". I replied, "I love you too Bob" That was the last I said to Bob. I hugged Loralyn and left. A few hours later, Bob died.

But he wasn't gone. It's hard to describe, but Bob and I continued a dialogue until his memorial a couple of weeks later. Often, it would come in a sensation, like his presence. I would Say, "Hi Bob". And he would answer, "Hey Charlie". "How is it there?"" It's just like you said, there's no pain, and it's wonderful! It's really great here, and I have a new body. Can't wait to see you again, brother." Once I was on a plane to Phoenix, afraid. Bob was there saying, "You don't need to be afraid, you're not sick like you were before, you can sleep without worry." It seemed that Bob was there with me until I said goodbye.

March 4, 2012 was a typical spring day in Half Moon Bay. Beautiful, warm Chamber of Commerce weather as the townspeople gathered to fellowship in Bob's Memorial Service. I was asked to recite from Bob's favorite Book, and it was good to see the whole community turn out. At the end of the ceremony, we said a prayer, and a flock of birds flew away and Bob was gone. I think his spirit stayed around until the Service, and upon conclusion, he was free to go. It is my hope that he hears this passage and knows my time is not long here, and that I will be with him soon.

Peter Bland

Peter Bland and his wife moved to Half Moon Bay in early 2000, and he met Charlie because they were both members of the 12-Step Recovery group, where you get to know people well without even knowing their last names.

When Charlie had his illness in 2011, Peter found out through friends within the group meetings. He understood Charlie's prognosis was poor from the outset. Certainly, he was expected to die, if not from pneumonia, then from the sepsis.

Peter worked for one of the biggest biotech companies in the industry. One of the hardest challenges was that they've never been able to come up with a drug for sepsis. The fact that Charlie survived was amazing.

Also, Peter attended one of the recovery meetings that people arranged to have at the hospital with Charlie. Even though Charlie and Peter were politically and socially different, when you're in that program and that kind of spiritual life, they are always looking out for the other people. They always want what's best for them always.

It's not uncommon for people in recovery, if they

grew up in a religious environment, to think the God of their understanding failed them. In Peter's case, when he was twelve, he fired his higher power of the Catholic Church that he grew up with. Instead, he took up alcohol as a capable substitute.

"When you get into the program," Peter told the group one day, "you must find the higher power of your understanding. The higher power of my understanding is more expansive than what the Catholic Church professes what God is. I can't ignore quantum physics and the other mysteries of what we've learned in the last hundred years. My interpretation of what I claim is my higher power differs much from my childhood understanding.

"I got sober in 1987, and my conception of my higher power in 2017 is much different than I understood in 1987 and had grown over the thirty years. Of the 12 Steps, one is to practice these principles in all of our affairs."

Besides working at a biotech company, Peter had been a musician his whole life. By the time he got sober, he was in New Wave bands in the eighties when the sound was new. The people in the New Wave movement were pretty negative. There was a lot of heroin and the bad attitudes, which mirrored the family of his upbringing, were prevalent. They say that we seek what we are comfortable or familiar with.

After Peter became sober in the late eighties, he left the music scene for ten years. The reason was very practical. When he tried to get involved, the group members took him to a rehearsal hall in downtown Oakland that smelled of beer and cigarettes. The smell, atmosphere, and activities were too familiar, and, rightly so, he knew he could not be around there.

It was not until the late 1990s when he started making music again. He became involved in a folk group and started writing music. His skill level improved over time. For years, he had become very frustrated and angry with the people he played with. The atmosphere, filled with egocentrism, had goals based around adulation as opposed to a higher goal with more merit.

About that same time, Peter auditioned for the Oakland Interfaith Gospel Choir. He was a tenor and was called back the same day. The first song they learned during the first night of rehearsal was Let Go and Let God. Being a member in recovery for twenty years, Peter laughed and genuinely appreciated the synchronicity. Okay, he got it.

It was agreed that members of the choir were to help promote the concerts. Peter and his wife and were active in sponsoring events associated with the Oakland Interfaith Youth Choir for teenagers. The reason he stuck with this was because he was saying yes to his higher power. The choir's mission statement was to bring joy to people through African American gospel music because that's what music was all about.

African American spirituals and work songs are inspiring. Imagine the attitude and perseverance required for a slave to live through slavery. If you ever listen to an African American spiritual, there is no negativity in it. Or, the song is an Old Testament story with a hidden message. The music brings a positive and optimistic message, which few of people have access to in their darkest times.

About a year after Charlie was out of the hospital, Peter pushed him to attend a concert in Half Moon Bay. Peter had a gut feeling that after all Charlie had been through, he would enjoy being part of this show as a co-host.

There was one spiritual musical arrangement the choir performed called, Lord, Hear My Prayer. Charlie came to the concert, and it blew him away. He said that one song just floored him because when he was in a coma, and he had his near-death experience, this is what I heard. That was how it felt. That was how it sounded.

Charlie's words rewarded the hearts of the singers, who worked hard to get this sound perfected. Even more rewarding was when the listener makes their connection to a higher power. Peter wanted this music to play a healing role in Charlie's life.

Still Digesting the Experience

Discussions with friends reminded Charlie often that it wasn't his time to die. Or, perhaps, God had something bigger planned. Those comments left Charlie wondering, because one point was clear to him.

He came back from the "going to the Light" experience because he heard Kyla crying.

When Charlie doubted himself, he took to praying each night while relaxing in his Jacuzzi. Water therapy relaxed the tension of the hips and helped him to sleep. Sometimes, the quizzical questions seemed to weigh heavy on Charlie's mind: Why did you send me back, God? Just make it clear to me. I am willing and ready to serve you.

Every time a friend reminded Charlie that God had a plan, and it was a good plan, he reiterated the fact almost every night. He felt overwhelmingly grateful because in recovery, some of the best prayers are offered at 2 am on one's knees in the bathroom. Sweating and shaking, one can still remember the simple prayer of God, please help me. And those are great prayers.

Charlie had faith that God was working His plan for Charlie even though he wasn't realizing it sometimes. Then, he felt it was starting to be revealed in little ways. For example, one day Kerri called and said, "Hey, Kyla's playing in water polo this afternoon over at the high school. Do you want to go?"

"Well, I can't walk yet. Still limited to the sofa."

"You have a wheelchair Charlie. I'll come get you and get you loaded and take you over there."

"Oh great. Yeah, let's go." Charlie went to the high school water polo game. Sometimes, scary thoughts crept in: Don't get me close to the water. I can't swim yet. If I fall in, I'll be in big trouble.

Kerri understood he was still feeling overwhelmed after all the trauma he experienced. She replied in kind, "No, we'll get you over here and you'll be fine." Feeling safe in that spot, Charlie watched his daughter interacting with her friends and frolicking and playing before her water polo match. Joy filled his heart. He cheered her on during the game, "Kyla, score that goal!" Charlie got a lot of joy out of seeing her having fun.

Suddenly, Charlie had the revelation. My God, this is what I came back for—to experience these moments of my daughter living life. That's why Charlie heard her when she was crying. Charlie came back to experience and support the strength of his two children's characters in this beautiful tapestry of life.

He knew he was here to help. He remembered that his love for people uplifted their spirits. He felt that the life experience he was having was like a painters' brushstroke. Each life experience was a unique mystery that could not be fully appreciated until the painting was almost finished. That life itself was a beautiful, fragile tapestry of intricate designs of our experiences.

Inevitably, Charlie became aware of making the most of this moment, every moment.

To appreciate the moment.
To participate in the moment.
To live in the moment.
Right here. Right Now.

Recently, Charlie went through some of the best of times, and some of the most challenging times of his life.

He accepted a new promotion and got engaged. The couple had planned a new life together in the Pacific Northwest, but it was not to be. Both partners needed to be willing to work through the inevitable difficulties that would arise, and he thought they had discussed how they would deal with issues. Charlie felt crushed when that relationship ended. He turned down the promotion to re-locate, sensing the need to stay near his home and community. He realized that it might not be the best career move, but as often happens, God was working in his life in ways he did not know. He told his friends that he felt God had something big in store for him. He was willing to walk in faith toward whatever that was.

In November of 2016, Charlie was laid off from work.

After a period of unemployment, and sitting on his hands in fear and sometimes just not drinking, Charlie received a phone call from a former co-worker looking for help and offering a tremendous opportunity to do exactly what he always loved. He readily accepted the offer and, at this moment, is having the time of his life in a career that he has always loved. Charlie also developed new friends to augment his friends in recovery that are focused on healthy lifestyles and personal development.

Celebrating the new job – Kian, Kyla, Jasper, Baylee & Charity ■

Relationships

Charlie always has a special time with each of the twins, Kian and Kyla, and was dedicated to their relationships and activities. For instance, Charlie took Kyla shopping one day before she went back to school. He once told her, "You know, you've never been treated as well as you deserve to be treated. I know you worry about having enough money, and that your brother has been getting his way a lot because of his hockey pursuits. But today is your day, we're going to go shopping, and you can get anything you want. We'll shop as long as you want. I'll stay here with you until you're done, even if it takes all day. So, this is your special day."

At the end of the day, Kyla was beaming and smiling. Charlie wanted her to know the feeling of being cherished, and he shared with her, "One day you will find a guy that's going to treat you well. You deserve to have that expectation, Kyla. Expect it because you deserve it."

On December 23, 2011 after Charlie took the twins to see a movie, they were driving home about 10 pm on a dark night. Charlie was tired, and they were driving home through Devil's Slide, where he had the accident that almost killed him earlier, of all places. Much had changed since Charlie's accident. The highway was wider and was housed in a tunnel to prevent people from sliding off the cliff into the Pacific Ocean.

They were driving through the tunnel. Kyla was listening to music on her iPod. The sounds of silence prompted Charlie to ask Kian a long question, "Everyone knows that

Charlie and Kyla shopping ■

one of the reasons I came back was when you both came to say goodbye to me. Kyla was crying, and I heard that. What I don't know is what you said to me when you had your special time alone?"

"Well Dad, that's easy. Remember when we went to the San Jose Sharks game. They were in the playoffs with the Colorado Avalanche, and it was a real nail biter. The game was tied and went into overtime. San Jose hit the shot in overtime to win the game in the playoffs, and the whole place went nuts. Everybody was jumping up and down and screaming. You turned, looked at me, and said, 'Son, always remember this moment.' That's what I was telling you, Dad. I will always remember that moment because it was such a special moment. I'll remember that for the rest of my life. That's what I was telling you about when I was saying goodbye."

Author Note: Now, you may realize why I titled this book Always Remember This Moment.

Why did I come back?

So, I could always remember that moment.

So, I could relish these moments that I'm still having.

So, I could feel trust and be assured of my relationship with God.

Pastor Paul expressed the transformation well. He said, "You know, Charlie is still the same guy. He's still the big, lovable, teddy bear. He's generous. He gives, and gives, and keeps on giving because that's what brings him joy. Most of all, Charlie has this sense of assurance—this sense that he knows there's a place to go to after we're done with this life, which is talked about in that song Hear My Prayer. Charlie tells it each year when he introduces the Oakland interfaith Gospel Choir singing that song that, "I am living, positive proof of the power of prayer."

By the way, the title of the movie they went to see when Kian told his dad to always remember this moment was *The Hobbit: An Unexpected Journey* in 3D. ■

EPILOGUE

Prince William County Virginia
August 29, 1862

Sunrise. Daybreak promised to bring another oppressive day of heat and humidity. Late August could be a treacherous thing, alternating chilly nights, with sweltering heat and humidity by day. The mist was rising off the dew, the crickets had begun their chirping against a backdrop of chicadas which sang throughout the night. Captain Ansley Moses awoke, dog-tired from the action of yesterday, but what a day it had been ! Complete victory ! The opposing army had been surprised at the little town of Manassas, completely overwhelmed. The supply depot had been captured, vital supplies seized, and everything burned to the ground. Such were the days of War.

It was earily quiet this morning, dead quiet only punctuated by an occassional rifle shot from a sentry, or a lost participant. That broke the stillness, stillness that once broke even caused the crickets to stop, but only momentarily. Captain Ansley (as his men called him) heard none of this, having been a veteran of this War since October of last year. He stirred, and sauntered rather gingerly over to the Company campfire, sore, and his ears still ringing from the battle the day before. Two of his men from Company D had been killed in the fight, and Ansley grieved for the families of his brave men back home.

General Lee had split his army with an unanticipated tactic, sent General Thomas (Stonewall) Jackson and his army on a flanking maneuver around General John Poe's Union

Forces who had been watching each other for some time across the Rappahannock River. Knowing General George McClelland of the North was sending reinforcements from nearby Washington DC, Lee decided to strike first. Therefore General Jackson, Captain Ansley Moses, and the whole of the Georgia 53rd Regiment, Company D, CSA went to the 2nd battle of Bull Run.1

Ansley Moses had been born April 9, 1829 two miles from Senoia, Georgia, a rural town southeast of Atlanta, and was raised on a farm near Turin, Georgia. He became a farmer and a teacher. A hard worker, and a man of noble character, Ansley built for himself a home on a large plantation in 1857 between Turin and Sharpsburg. Ansley was strong in his belief and faith in God, and it seemed God favored him with His blessings. Ansley married Mary Leavell and settled into a pastoral lifestyle.

The War Between the States broke out on April 12, 1861 at Ft. Sumter, South Carolina as most southern states seceded from the Union. Ansley at first opposed secession, but when Georgia broke away, Ansley helped organize a local militia into the 53rd Regiment, enlisted October 25, 1861 and was quickly appointed Captain of Company D.

The smell of chicory coffee and campfire punctuated the air as Captain Ansley sought his first debriefing of the day, for a battlefield victory, the losses seemed unsustainable, but news that General Pope of the North had turned his Army to counterattack required immediate action on the part of the Regiment, so the Captain issued orders to effect what is termed today as guerrilla warfare, and Company D melted into the surrounding woods. Pope's Federals showed up that morning as expected, but the maneuver by Jackson's Army confused the enemy, and made it difficult to locate the Confederates. Ultimately the battle ensued, and losses were heavy that day on both sides. Captain Ansley Moses led his men bravely and fought through the day, holding their position against numerically superior forces until additional rebels under the command of General James Longstreet showed up around noon to reinforce General Jackson and Captain Moses' flank. Although General Pope was known as a braggart by reputation, and disliked by many Union officers, when faced with what he believed was the entire Army of Northern Virginia, he ordered the retreat across Bull Run and back toward Washington.

The Union retreat cast a pallor over the North, in particular that the Union was undergoing a crisis of leadership, confidence in the new President was low, and there was constant infighting and posturing as politics pervaded the decisions being made. It seemed the South had the advantage with a very charismatic President, and a commanding General that was both well respected and loved by the troops. General Robert E. Lee was a West Point graduate, and extremely well experienced in battle and military tactics. But a chill rippled through the populace as the Army of Northern Virginia was only 26 miles as the crow flies from downtown Washington DC. Preparations were soon underway to evacuate the City as it had been in 1812, and discussions were held whether to relocate to Philadelphia or New York.

General Lee decided to seize the moment of opportunity and press forward. Word soon came down to the Georgians to move out. "Pack up boys, we're headin' North to win this War!" exclaimed Captain Ansley. The Army of Northern Virginia moved north with the goal of cutting the rail lines to Washington and securing supplies for the Confederate forces. By September 17th, President Lincoln had recalled General McClelland to protect Washington and the newly formed Army of the Potomac clashed with the Southern forces near Sharpsburg, MD at Antietam Creek. The Battle of Antietam was the single bloodiest day in American History with both sides suffering over 23,000 casualties. Captain Ansley Moses of the 53rd Georgia Regiment Company D was there.

Attempting to counter the threat, Lincoln removed General McClelland, and shortly afterward Union General Ambrose Burnside planned to move south towards the Confederate capital at Richmond via Fredricksburg, but the ill-conceived plan began to quickly deteriorate. First of all, the pontoon bridges needed to ford the Rappahannock River did not arrive on time, and when they did, indecisiveness of the part of Burnside who refused to grant the supplications of his subordinates to cross the river, due to his fear they would be washed out in the rising waters. Meanwhile, General Lee's Army (along with the Georgia Regiment) moved into the high ground above Fredricksburg, and the result was a massacre of the invading Northerners on December 13th.

After that event, Captain Moses and his men were ordered to engage the North in a series of tactical maneuvers and flanking operations through the woods at Chancellorsville. Burnside had been replaced by Major General Joseph Hooker who decided to rest and replenish his Army through the cold winter months and prepare for a spring offensive. Lee once again split his inferior force and General Stonewall Jackson and the 53rd Georgia Regiment circled 12 miles out of the way and emerged from the woods at 5:30 pm on May 2. The Confederates smashed into the Union XI Corps completely destroying their line and forcing retreat. While this battle was considered Lee's greatest victory, it also came at his greatest cost as General Thomas (Stonewall) Jackson was shot while inspecting the lines by friendly fire. Having his arm amputated, Jackson died of pneumonia (possibly Sepsis) on May 10.

After the victory at Chancellorsville, the Confederate Army marched unmolested into Pennsylvania, heading toward Philadelphia and ultimate victory. Captain Ansley knew the rebels were vastly outnumbered, he just hoped that the recent victories would scare the politicians in Washington DC just enough to sue for peace, and end this War he had been living the last 2 years. As you can imagine, life was very difficult on the road in a battle for your life nearly every week. Food and clothing were at a premium, but the emotional strain was staggering.

On July 1, 1863, Lee's Army ran into what seemed like a small skirmish at a crossroads town named Gettysburg in Pennsylvania. The next day the Confederates attacked heavily on the left and right with heavy casualties, and by day 3, the group of Georgians from the 53rd Regiment Company D joined in the fray as Lee sent a small contingent into the center to pierce the Union line which they did briefly but eventually failed. "Pickett's Charge" went down in history as of the bravest assaults in military history, and which is widely recognized as the turning point in the War. Both the North and the South suffered astronomical losses, Captain Ansley lost his superior officer and good friend Lt. Col. J.W. Hance, and Lee's Army turned back to protect the South.

Captain Ansley followed General Lee and General James Longstreet back through Virginia and into Tennessee that fall and participated in the Battle of Chickamauga, on September 19-20, 1863 and became the new record for sustained losses on both sides with over 20,000 casualties. Nearby Chattanooga was laid siege by the Confederates as the North had setup a supply center for their planned invasion of the Deep South. General Longstreet was ordered north to reinforce Knoxville by General Braxton Bragg, as President Abraham Lincoln ordered General Sherman to Knoxville to reinforce Gen. Ambrose Burnside. The result was a clash of the armies on November 29, 1863 when Captain Ansley Moses was wounded, taken prisoner and shipped off to Ft. Delaware.

Ft. Delaware November 1863

Ft. Delaware was initially built to be a protector of ports around Wilmington, but was soon transformed into prison camp in the spring of 1862. Not originally designed to be a prison, its accommodations were transformed to house numerous detainees including Union deserters. When the commander of the Fort was informed that he would be receiving prisoners, he protested to Washington that the Fort had no room to house them, he was then curtly ordered to "find room".

Additional barracks were hastily erected in early 1863, but were less than adequate. The construction was such that the facilities were supposed to house up to 10,000 prisoners, and was so drafty that it was freezing cold in the winter, and stifling hot in the summer. Prisoners were allotted only a thin overcoat and a cheap blanket, and otherwise had to fend for themselves. The food supplied consisted of 2 half-rations a day, usually watered down soup with worms and a bite of stringy meat. Starvation rations and clothes which did little to ward off the cold resulted in many prisoners succumbing to disease, and eventually death.

When Captain Ansley Moses arrived with grievous wounds from the battlefield at Knoxville, a new hospital had just been completed. The prisoner ranks had swelled to over 12,000 and the conditions continued to deteriorate. Once the hospital was completed, it housed from 200-700 soldiers each month with a plethora of disease and sickness. Ansley was one of those, and was billeted with the enlisted men in the barracks while even though an officer, wanted to be close with the men of his Regiment. It was also a better chance to escape.

Although several hundred prisoners did escape, often by jumping through the privy holes, the fate of Captain Ansley Moses was to suffer through to the bitter end. A handwritten newspaper, Prison Times, reported on the activities taking place in the Prison, and an issue in April 1865 made the comment, "A thousand ill; twelve thousand on an island which should hold four; the general level three feet below low water mark, twenty deaths a day of dysentery and the living having more life on them than in them. Occasional lack of water and thus a Christian (!) nation treats the captives of its sword." Thus went the two years of hell he spent in a POW camp.

Newnan, Georgia 1865

The Civil war officially ended on April 9, 1865 with the surrender by General Lee at Appomattox Courthouse. In typical military efficiency, Captain Ansley Moses was not released from Ft. Delaware until June 12, 1865 after taking an Oath of Allegiance. Turned out on dry land, he then began the long walk home from Delaware to Georgia. After many months of being one of the "soldiers in gray", returning from the War, now civilian Ansley Moses made the arduous journey to find his homeland in catastrophic ruin.

All around the greater Atlanta area, and virtually all the way to Savannah was laid waste by General William Tecumseh Sherman and his infamous "March to the Sea." Virtually everything was destroyed and Ansley experienced more anguish than he had the entire duration of the War. But apparently God didn't bring him this far to drop him on his head, by the time he arrived home, he was surprised to see that his home still stood!

Home life in the South during the War was no picnic either. Mary Ann Leavell Moses was left to run the plantation, and rear 5 children at the same time. With all the men away at War, a prodigy of service was rendered unrecognized by the loyal servant leaders. Some slaves were so loyal to their white families they took on some of the more manly chores of the day, and the white matriarchs rose to the occasion by necessity, and through indomitable will. Such was the household in the Moses family. Mary Leavell Moses and her trusted Foreman Samuel Moses (as most slaves took the family name) worked the farm until the Yankees came.

Samuel Moses was of such fine character that he was respected by the townspeople in Newnan, Georgia when he would go into town to get supplies for "Miss 'Mary'", he would be greeted and welcomed as any freeman would be at that time. Sam, like a lot of the slaves of that era had no place to go upon emancipation, and be it trust or shrewdness on all parties, a lot of freed slaves stayed on and helped share-crop the farms. It was written of Sam (and Captain Ansley) that "They came no Finer" and many articles were published in the Newnan newspapers attesting to Sam Moses' character and the respect he garnered in the community2.

Although there are no known historical records to substantiate the rumor, it was widely accepted by the family that the indomitable will of Mary Leavell Moses, is what saved the plantation from burning and pillaging by Sherman's Army. It is said that she and Sam Moses, upon hearing of the imminent approach by the north, gathered up all the slaves and others at the plantation and formulated a plan. "Now I know ya'll been hearin' of all this destruction being wrecked upon us by this terrible Army descendin' upon our land", said Mary Leavell to the group. "And we've all been hearin' the rumors of what these soldiers are doin' to our women folk, stealing our animals, and burnin' everythin', but here's what I want ya'll to do. Take this Strawberry Jam ah've been puttin' up, and when them damn Yankees come upon us, spread it all over your faces and arms, and they will believe we have the Pox, and leave us alone!" Apparently it worked, the house was left unscathed, and the folks and animals of the Moses plantation were left unmolested.

When Captain Ansley Moses arrived back in Newnan, he and the entire area was faced with the daunting challenge of reconstruction. The community came to Ansley and asked that since they had no schools, would he volunteer to teach their children as they had nowhere to go. Ansley responded that since he was to infirmed by his war injuries, if the parents would send their children to his house, he would teach them from his bed upstairs. So began what would later become the Newnan Male Academy, and a legacy of teaching and education for generations to come. Ansley and Mary Leavell were to make do their remaining years, raise their 5 children, one of which, Charles Leavell Moses would go on to serve as the Georgia representative to the U.S. Congress, and help the South recover during the period known as Reconstruction.

After all Ansley Moses had been through, two years of constant warfare, two years of POW Camp, walking home from Delaware wounded and emaciated, enduring Reconstruction, Captain Ansley Moses passed away on September 16, 1886 at the age of 57. ∎

• Cause of Death: Bronchial Pneumonia (Sepsis?)

• Ansley Moses was my Great Great Grandfather.

*1   *http://www.history.com/topics/american-civil-war/second-battle-of-bull-run*

"2 *http://wgnewspap ers.galileo.usg.edu/wgnewspapers/view?docId=bookreader%2Fnhd%2Fnhd1921%2Fnhd1921-0407.mets.xml%3Bquery%3D%22uncle+sam+moses%22%3Bbrand%3Dwgnewspapers-j2k-brand#page/1/mode/1up*

ACKNOWLEDGEMENTS

"At the end of the day, it's not about what you have or even what you've accomplished. It's about what you've done with those accomplishments. It's about who you've lifted up, who you've made better. It is about what you've given back".
—Denzel Washington, A Hand to Guide Me

There are too many little miracles to acknowledge, but the heroes stand out on their own. My former wife, Kerri, you were stellar. Thank you for bringing the twins in daily and keeping them in the loop on what was going on. You guys dealt with the real trauma.

I am grateful for my churches, the one I attend in Half Moon Bay, and that church of my childhood in Chattanooga, Tennessee. Also, the Oakland Interfaith Gospel Choir helped to show me, beyond all doubt, that I am living proof of the power of prayer.

My heartfelt thanks to Natalie, my physical therapist, and Laurie, my occupational therapist. You helped to save my life just as surely as any of the medical treatment that was contributed.

I like to say I don't have many close friends, but for those that I do have, we love each other beyond words. My deepest gratitude to Roger Berry, Bill and Rena Bassett, Tom and Lisa Hanley, and the "One Eyed-Ding Dong" Meagan Hanley, who was so worried about rubbing my feet, but overwhelmed with joy when I made it to the Hanley's house for Thanksgiving.

Dave Hazen, Richard Raine, Patti Llamas, and the employees of Kiewit Infrastructure West, you were the best. No other company is so invested in the well-being of their employees to the extent Kiewit is, and Dave Hazen is a leader who walks his talk.

My deepest gratitude goes to my brothers: Tommy, Chris, and Ellis. Mom was right. She did raise us to care for each other. We did our best to console her that we would be all right once she was gone. This sepsis recovery proved beyond measure that the Gardner brothers share a bond born in love. This brotherly love was passed to the next generation as nephew Charlton took a week shift caring for "Cool Uncle Charlie."

To all the women I loved, and loved me in return, you will always hold a special place in my heart and in my memories. Thank you for the experiences, the lessons learned, and spending part of your life with me.

I would be remiss if I didn't acknowledge my spiritual guides. Formerly of First Presbyterian Church in Chattanooga, the Reverend Ben Haden taught me forgiveness as God taught David in the Bible. Pastor Paul Richardson who recognized the importance of smuggling in "In-and-Out" burgers and shakes. When I was thirsty, he gave me food and drink! Steve Arterburn of New Life Ministries for writing the Foreword and for guiding our tour of the Holy Land. Thanks to you and Larry Sonnenburg, I will never hear another sermon or read the Bible the same way again.

My first sponsor John Gale, who walked me through the 12-Steps of recovery and showed me that I can have not only a second chance at life, but also a chance at a second life. This journey has been absolutely amazing! My current sponsor Steve Wilson, who has helped guide me through life and relationship challenges as a sponsor, lawyer, and co-executor of my meager estate.

Oh, and the latest of miracles, remember that house on the golf course Ellis pointed out that would be perfect for me? I bought it this past September. It turns out the 17th hole was where my dad shot his one and only hole in one, and I promised to come back there someday and do the same. So, dad, if you're watching, I'm coming back!

And last but not least, the guys I get to work with in recovery: Nate, Rich, Joey, Steve, John, and Eben in Northern California. Roger, Eddie & Christine, Creaters, Fusco, Scott, Glenn and all of the North Scottsdale Fellowship where my journey began.

Thank you for keeping me sober and alive these last 20 years.

...and don't forget...
Always Remember this Moment!

◆

ABOUT THE AUTHOR

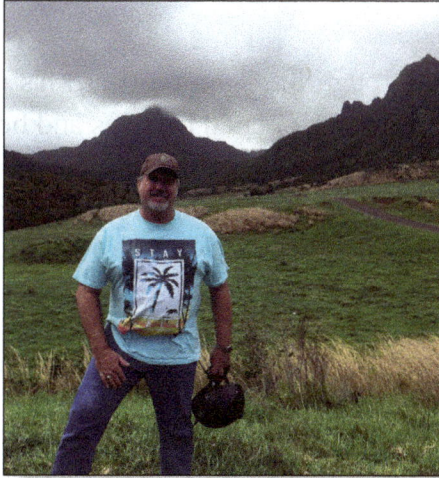

If you think science can explain everything, then think again. Charles Gardner, an engineer whose whole life and career was based upon measurable and observable facts is not the person you would expect to have such an extraordinary experience, and certainly not the person you would expect to tell the whole world.

Charles had a great career, good friends and a loving family-everything a person could really want. But he was struck by tragedy, circumstances that would scare most people to death. In his case it did.

After a set of gruesome circumstances, Charles went into a six-week coma, vacillating between life and death. Science could not save him. His physical strength could not save him and it was miraculous that he even lived through the coma. Finally, after the decision was made to pull the plug and take him off life support, the only apparent means of keeping him alive, he died. But his death was very brief. As he floated up through the light, he heard his daughter cry. He then turned around, opened his eyes and began his road to recovery and his new life. Love brought him back to life when pure strength, medicine and science could not!

Charles shares his story about tragedy, survival, and recovery in a compelling way that will have you turning each page wanting more and engrossing you in the astounding details.

Charles lives in Tennessee. ■

www.ingramcontent.com/pod-product-compliance
Lightning Source LLC
Chambersburg PA
CBHW071844090426
42811CB00035B/2319/J